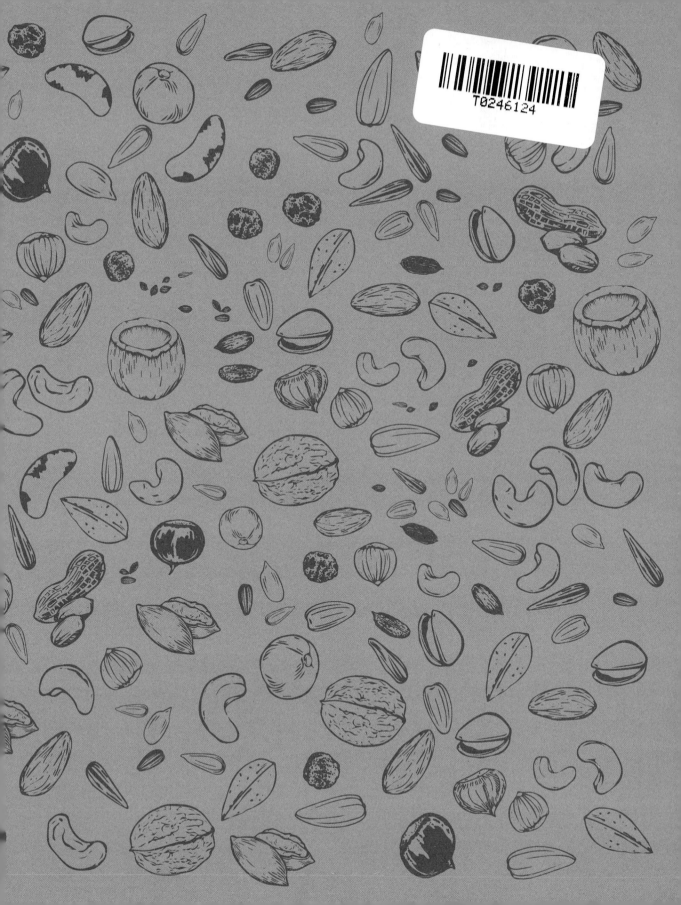

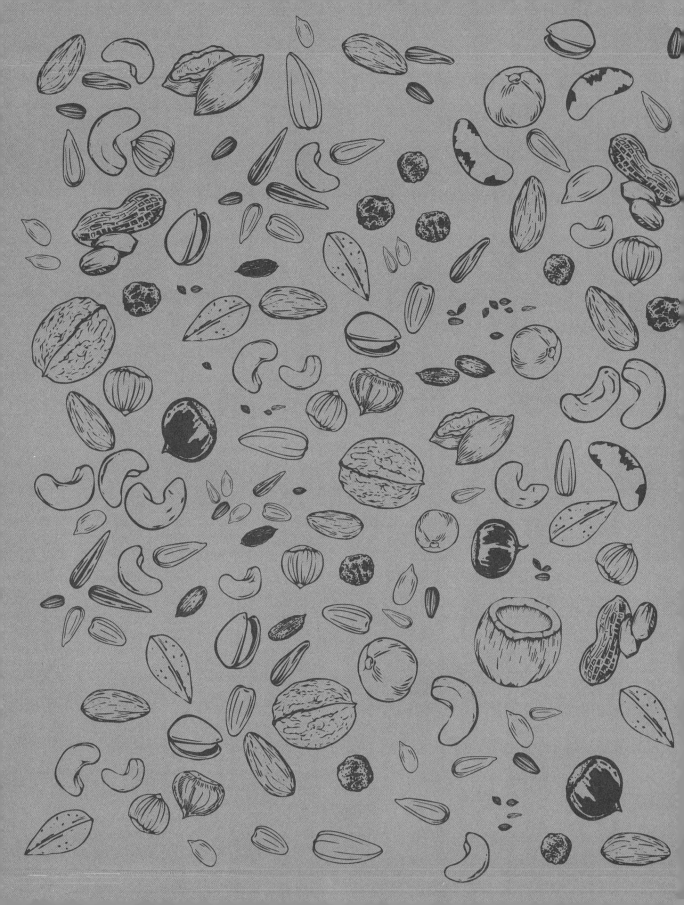

LET'S
GO
NUTS

Estella Schweizer
Photography: Winfried Heinze

LET'S GO NUTS

80 VEGAN RECIPES WITH NUTS AND SEEDS

PRESTEL

MUNICH · LONDON · NEW YORK

CONTENTS

NUT PROFILES

RECIPES

PREFACE

I'm nuts about nuts! That's what I tell people that are interested in these edible seeds contained in hard shells. And I think everyone should be similarly "nutty" because nuts are absolutely delicious.

We all know about nuts, but they are still greatly underrated by most of us. Nuts are so much more than a snack to munch on or an ingredient for Christmas baking. Beautifully crunchy, with a mild, slightly sweet flavor, nuts are incredibly versatile and suitable for use in all sorts of recipes. Nuts are also high in energy and very healthy. Just a handful of nuts each day brings health benefits because they are a source of important nutrients and can help prevent cardiovascular disease.

Our eating habits and food choices have a massive impact on the earth's habitat and nuts have a relatively good environmental footprint. But as I will discuss, their sustainable, value-added cultivation and fair trade are crucial to maintaining this.

Because I am so passionate about maximizing the potential of nuts in cooking, this book aims to coax them out of the shadows and into the limelight — where they rightfully belong! Along with their healthy properties, nuts possess exceptional texture and flavor that will improve your meals. Most of the time, I intentionally use nuts in small quantities to add the finishing touch to a recipe, but sometimes they should be the center of attention — for example, in hazelnut milk (recipe see p. 24), cashew quark (recipe see p. 25), or almond ricotta (recipe see p. 26). Nuts also play a leading role in my recipes for deconstructed lasagna with cashew béchamel (recipe see p. 172/173),

no cheese fondue (recipe see p. 225), and winter nut roast (recipe see p. 228/229).

In this book, I want nuts to come out of their shell to take you on a culinary voyage of discovery. After a short introduction, I share various basic recipes for nut milks and nut milk products, along with dressings, marinades, and sauces, followed by 67 recipes that take us on a culinary journey through the seasons, demonstrating just how simple and delicious plant-based cooking can be and how easy it is to incorporate nuts into our diet. My recipes are vegan and mostly gluten free, so they are great for everyone.

Between the recipes, you will find profiles of different nuts, listing useful information, health benefits, culinary tips, and a description of the environmental, economic, and social challenges that play a part in their cultivation and sale. You can seek out specific nuts, like a squirrel with its winter supplies, or leave these discoveries to chance, stumbling across them every so often while cooking. Finally, we look inside my pantry to see which foods I always have in stock, and I offer advice about what kitchen equipment I find most useful.

This book puts nuts in the spotlight and shows how they can be incorporated into everyday vegan cuisine. I am sure you are going to be a massive nut fan by the time we are done, and that nuts will enhance your everyday life in the same way they have mine.

Your inspiration starts here!
Estella Schweizer

WHY WE SHOULD EAT NUTS

As well as tasting fantastic, nuts and seeds are among the healthiest foods we can eat. In the nut profiles found later in the book, you will discover that the term "nut" does not refer to a cohesive botanical group; instead, it refers to any dry fruit with high protein and fat levels, and an impressively high micronutrient content. Also, while nuts and seeds are distinct, for the purposes of this book, I often use the term nut but am referring to both nuts and seeds.

Nuts are a genuine superfood and are particularly important in plant-based cuisine as a welcome source of protein. They contain minimal water and are packed with minerals, trace elements, lots of B-complex vitamins, and vitamin E. Eating just 30 to 40 grams per day is enough to cover 50 percent of your requirements for certain minerals. And all for an equivalent of just 10 to 15 percent of the recommended daily calorie intake for men and women.

Nuts and seeds mostly contain monounsaturated and polyunsaturated fatty acids, which help regulate our fatty acid metabolism and lower cholesterol. Thanks to their high proportion of dietary fiber and vitamin E, nuts also have anti-inflammatory properties. Eating nuts helps prevent the formation of arteriosclerotic plaques in blood vessels. Folic acid is often present in high quantities and this, combined with vitamins B2 and B6, can lower homocysteine levels in the blood, preventing the buildup of deposits on the arterial walls and offering protection for the coronary arteries. High levels of arginine also have a positive impact on heart health. These amino acids play a crucial role in the formation of nitric oxide, which relaxes the arterial wall musculature, resulting in lower blood pressure.

Contrary to widespread belief, nuts can even help you stay slim. They have a complex structure and supply lots of energy, which keeps you feeling full for longer. Large cross-sectional studies show that people who incorporate nuts in their meals eat fewer snacks than those who avoid nuts. Furthermore, nut eaters tend to eat less at subsequent meals than those who refrain from eating nuts.

Research shows that nuts have a beneficial impact on body weight despite their very high calorie content. One plausible reason for this is that the main fat contained in nuts cannot be absorbed as easily by the body as the energy from isolated fats, such as oil and vegan margarine, or low-quality carbohydrates like highly processed flour and refined sugar. This means some of the calories consumed with nuts are simply excreted without being absorbed. Nutritional experts also suggest that nuts are associated with metabolic thermogenesis. This is often referred to as the thermic effect, in which body temperature rises slightly after eating and excess energy is consumed by the heating process.

As you can see, these are all great reasons for substituting some of the oil in sauces, dressings, and spreads with nut butters, which taste fantastic and offer a more complex fat source with significantly more micronutrients. The nut profiles interspersed between the recipes in the book describe which nuts contain which vitamins and minerals, so you can find out what each nut is particularly suitable for and what you need to look out for when shopping.

THE BENEFITS OF PROCESSING NUTS WHERE THEY ARE GROWN

Nuts are highly coveted in vegan cooking thanks to the many nutrients they contain, but they are also a firm fixture in other dietary approaches and philosophies. Nuts are a delicious ingredient and a genuine superfood, even if they are not always the most local or sustainable option.

The plants that produce these edible seeds have varied requirements in terms of climate and soil conditions. They grow on all continents but particularly thrive in warmer regions, including countries in the Global South. This brings certain challenges for trade.

It is true that other regions have small local businesses dedicated to cultivating nuts, with nut trees in their orchards and on other arable land, and that these producers often sell their crops at weekly markets or in their own farm shops. However, for economic reasons, nuts from small local businesses do not generally make it to supermarkets.

The entire infrastructure around harvesting, processing, and sales has gradually relocated to wherever it is easiest to implement and wherever offers the greatest economic return. While this might be understandable from an economic perspective, there are sociological and environmental repurcussions. For example, more than half the cashews sold on the global market come from the African continent, but less than 5 percent are dried, shelled, and packed there. Instead, a majority of African cashews are taken in their shells by container ships to Asia, where they can be processed more cheaply, even though this is to the detriment of the producers. The less processing nuts have undergone, the lower the revenue. In fact, the amount that farmers receive for their raw goods is so small, most of them live below the poverty line. To be more specific, between 2018 and 2022, producers received around 1.50 Euros per kilo of unshelled cashews. A kilo of shelled, ready-to-eat cashews, on the other hand, was worth roughly 10 Euros.

A similar story applies for most other nuts. Producers stand to earn most if they can process (and/or refine) the nuts themselves for direct sale, but unshelled, unprocessed products are often bought from producers for very low prices before being sent to other countries for processing. If nuts take a detour via Asia, to be shelled and processed on an industrial scale (for example to make oil, or a refined product or snack) before being sold, the farmers see nothing of the additional income generated by their produce.

Unfortunately, this is far from being the only problem. Depending on location, nuts are either processed by machine (China and Vietnam) or by hand (India) and occupational health and safety is often neglected. Many of the predominantly female workers in India, who crack nuts with their bare hands for a low wage, suffer appalling skin injuries due to contact with a caustic oil contained in the shells that needs to be removed by heating the nuts before shelling.

In addition, transportation of nuts often results in excess emissions. While a cashew that is ready to eat and imported direct from Africa takes about 15 days to travel to Europe, by contrast, a non-fair trade nut that has been shipped to Asia to be shelled takes about 60 days and will have racked up many more kilometers.

This could not be further removed from the kind of trade that is best for humans and the environment. Fairness and sustainability are always best served by processing raw commodities in the country where they are grown. This allows producers to achieve higher profits, which then lay the foundation for supporting the livelihoods, health, and education of local families.

As consumers, we can send a clear signal by choosing fair trade produce and rejecting the tarnished conventional trading system. Products with the Fairtrade seal are produced in line with specific standards. In addition to environmentally friendly farming, a ban on hazardous pesticides, seed inspections, and a higher price for organically produced goods, Fairtrade certification also monitors economic and social criteria, such as transparent trade relations, regulated working conditions, the organization of democratic communities, and a ban on child labor. Wherever food is being grown in the world, a sustainable and forward-looking approach must be founded on sound economic, environmental, and social principles.

The fair trade situation for almonds, hazelnuts, walnuts, peanuts, and pistachios is slightly different from the other nuts in the book. These nuts are sometimes cultivated in countries in the Global South or other economically deprived regions, with support for cultivation, production, harvest, and trade from companies like Fair for Life that promote fair trade and have strict criteria to ensure producers get the best possible price. But these nuts are also grown in the Global North, in countries that have suitable climatic conditions and a cultural tradition that supports these farms.

Consumers have a responsibility to look more closely at product information, checking for compliance with organic farming standards and ensuring producers focus on protecting the environment and promoting sustainable soil health. Organic nuts, along with cereals, pulses, fruit, and vegetables, have a clear advantage in this regard. When shopping, we should pay attention to each product's country of origin, which is generally marked on the packaging, and favor companies that sell directly to the European and American market and support value-added cultivation.

In terms of cultivation, harvesting, and trade routes, chestnuts and seeds are less detrimental to people and the environment.

Even so, I still very much prefer organic produce for reasons relating to soil health, to avoid pollution and pesticide residues, and to do something good for our environment.

HOW TO USE THIS BOOK

COOKING WITH THE SEASONS

This book is designed around the seasons, with recipes that focus on the ingredients that are most readily available at each time of year. However, there is no getting away from the fact that our eating habits are often very far removed from the natural rhythm of the seasons. Nobody subsists exclusively on stored supplies of root vegetables, cabbage, and fermented or preserved produce between December and April. Most people don't go without tomatoes between October and June, nor do they deprive themselves of oranges and lemons between May and November. Even consumers with the most attentive eye for seasonal produce are inevitably faced with the complex reality of food production and retail structures. From early in the year, supermarket shelves fill up with colorful vegetables, herbs, and salads that have been cultivated in greenhouses or imported from warmer regions.

As far as possible, I try to purchase seasonal fruit, vegetables, salads, and herbs. Asparagus and rhubarb are only available in April, May, and June. Tomatoes are primarily a midsummer product. In summer and autumn, we find leafy lettuces, such as Batavia, Lollo Rosso, and butterhead on sale, while in the colder months, these varieties are replaced by lamb's lettuce, endive, and chicory.

In this book, each season is portrayed in a way that reflects its particular character, with a passion for good food being the common theme throughout the year. When the first green shoots appear in springtime, as a breeze blows and the sun glistens on leaves still coated with hoarfrost, we crave food that is fresh and crisp. Summer brings fabulously enticing salads and light, Mediterranean dishes, while autumn's rich harvest ushers a blaze of color to our plates. As the days get shorter in winter, and we are faced with chilly evenings and unappealing weather, our natural instinct is to seek out warmth and coziness with hearty, nourishing meals.

INDEPENDENCE AND THE JOY OF EXPERIMENTATION IN THE KITCHEN

My recipes are designed to boost creativity and can be adapted as desired. The aim is to give you a rough framework, a kind of basic outline. The emphasis on specific flavors and the quantities and combinations of ingredients are intended as suggestions to be modified to suit your preferences. The ultimate result should be your own work, guided by your favorite nuts, vegetables, grains, spices, and herbs and what you have available. Have confidence in your own taste.

You may find that some recipes lack specific instructions about how runny or thick a sauce should be, or whether an ingredient should be coarsely or finely ground. I have made a conscious choice to encourage you to experiment — after all, variety is the spice of life! I am constantly tweaking my own recipes, too. It's amazing what you can discover with some freedom in the kitchen.

Trust in your ability to adapt the recipes for each season and feel free to substitute different fruits and vegetables. In autumn, for example, you could serve tender, steamed broccoli instead of roasted asparagus with the mango and peanut salsa (recipe see p. 65). In winter, you could substitute roasted Brussels sprouts. In summer, the nut roast with chestnuts (recipe see p. 228/229) can be transformed into a Mediterranean bake by replacing the mushrooms and other vegetables with eggplant and zucchini and using chopped tomato instead of chestnuts. The saffron risotto (recipe see p. 222/223) could be served with green asparagus, squash, or roasted carrots instead of puntarelle, and the oven-roasted bell pepper and apricot salad (recipe see p. 114) works beautifully with kale, roasted parsnips, or sautéed young Swiss chard.

If you are not a fan of buckwheat, the buckwheat and mushroom risotto (recipe see p. 175) can easily be made using Arborio rice or spelt. If you don't have any millet, try using quinoa for the artichokes with hazelnut mayonnaise (recipe see p. 124/125), and if you can't track down Beluga lentils in the supermarket, the lentil and apple salad to go with the roasted beets (recipe see p. 166) can just as easily be made using brown or green lentils, or even kidney beans.

I hope these examples help demonstrate how freely you should interpret my recipes and how independent you should be in using your own preferences to guide you as you conjure up colorful veggie dishes in your kitchen. My cooking philosophy is about simplicity, pragmatism, and autonomy.

DIETARY PREFERENCES AND INGREDIENTS

As already mentioned elsewhere, I mainly use organic ingredients. As well as being environmentally friendly, protecting soil health, and so on, there is another key factor behind my preference for organic farming: the taste. That's more important than anything in a cookbook, don't you think?

Organically cultivated foods taste more natural and have a more intense, rounded flavor. The full-bodied flavor of these ingredients improves the taste of my everyday meals so much that I just cannot bring myself to use conventional products anymore. In fact, I buy all the pantry foods for my daily cooking — grains, pulses, nuts, soy products, oils, spices — from organic or zero-waste stores. For convenience, I always have a few supplies ready. But be careful — there's no need to go mad with your hoarding and stockpiling! Make sure you only buy things you genuinely love to eat and will use regularly. It would be a terrible shame to end up throwing food away after it has been squirrelled in the furthest corners of your cupboards, only to be rediscovered months or years later once it has gone off.

I like to source my vegetables, salad greens, herbs, and fruit from my local weekly market. If you shop regularly at a market, you will get to know the local suppliers and soon figure out which stalls have the best produce. Not all local food producers will be organically certified, even if their production methods are in line with organic standards. This is because the certification process is often expensive and time-consuming for small businesses. Talk to food producers to find out how they work. This will help you avoid harmful pesticides or other residues on the food you buy.

The recipes in this book are vegan and most are also gluten free. There are both animal welfare and human rights arguments for a vegan diet — after all, humans are involved in livestock farming and abattoirs. Those doing the gruesome work in intensive farming are certainly being exploited, but so are those who feel the distinct impact of these global interdependencies on the other side of the world. For me, a plant-based diet is the only viable option for a greener future in terms of climate policy and protecting the environment. Indeed, this may be the only way to safeguard a worthwhile future on this planet.

INTERPRETING THE RECIPES

Before we get started, there are a couple more things to note about the recipes. I assume that fruits, vegetables, herbs, and salad greens are always washed well before use. I only peel ingredients if absolutely necessary. Unless the skin is blemished, I even leave it on beets, sweet potatoes, and Hokkaido squash. It is particularly important to focus on organic ingredients if you are going to eat the skin on vegetables and citrus fruit.

I use the convection setting on my oven. This saves energy compared with the non-convection setting, as you don't have to set the oven temperature as high. But if you prefer to cook in a non-convection oven, just increase the specified oven temperature by 20°C. That will work fine, too.

When I'm cooking something in a saucepan or skillet, I generally heat the oil and sauté the vegetables, etc. briskly over high heat at first. Then I continue cooking over a low to moderate heat, often with the lid on.

I assume almost every kitchen is equipped with basics, such as parchment paper, a balloon whisk, vegetable peeler, mandoline, grater, chopping board, and a couple of knives. With this in mind, the kitchen equipment section of each recipe only lists the more unusual items.

Learn more about my personal pantry items, my favorite foods, and my everyday kitchen equipment from page 246.

THE THEORY AND PRACTICE OF COOKING WITH NUTS

With just a few tips and tricks, you can make nuts and seeds part of your daily diet and find easy ways to incorporate them into your cooking and baking. You'll soon get the hang of this approach and make it part of your everyday routine.

SOAKING

If you want to make your own nut milk, yogurt, quark, or cream cheese, it is best to soak the nuts in water for at least four (ideally eight) hours or overnight before using. Just put the nuts in a bowl or jar and cover with cold water. After soaking, they can be drained in a sieve, rinsed thoroughly in cold water, and then processed as required using fresh water.

Soaked nuts are easier to chop in the food processor and will be creamier. The soaking process washes away dust and colorings, so whatever you are making with the nuts will also be slightly paler.

Soaking also initiates the germination process. This helps activate the nutrients in the nuts, allowing them to be absorbed more easily by the body. At the same time, some of the naturally occurring phytic acid in the nuts is broken down, which aids digestion. As long as you are not sensitive to phytic acid, you can continue to enjoy crunchy, unsoaked nuts.

FERMENTATION

To use nuts to make yogurt, cream cheese, quark, etc., the basic mixture must first be allowed to mature. This maturation process is called fermentation and refers to the decomposition caused by bacterial or yeast cultures. During maturation, these cultures break down starches into small sugar components and proteins into individual amino acids. This creates probiotic bacteria and carbon dioxide, which feed our microbiome when consumed, promoting excellent digestive and intestinal health.

Fermentation also affects the flavor of food and prolongs its shelf life. At the same time, it ensures nutrients and vitamins are more readily available to the body and easier to digest. Fermented products develop a pleasant acidity (such as found in yogurt, quark, and cream cheese) or even an aromatic flavor (such as found in cashew Camembert, miso, tempeh, and natto).

Once you have made the basic substance to be fermented, you add a probiotic "starter culture," mixing it in thoroughly until everything is well combined. Next you leave the nut milk product at room temperature to mature for 8–12 hours. The fermentation process is clearly visible thanks to the little bubbles that form in the mixture. During fermentation, the basic nut cream mixture develops an acidic flavor and undergoes changes to its structure and volume.

There are several reasons why fermentation might initially be unsuccessful or even go too far. Crucial factors include insufficient or excess probiotic, an initial temperature for the basic mixture that is too high or too low, as well as the ambient temperature. Sometimes no fermentation at all takes place, which could be because the chosen probiotic culture was not sufficiently potent. Patience and practice are required. But with just a bit of experience and a readiness to experiment, you can get excellent results. Let's get cracking!

Probiotic cultures

Probiotics are living microorganisms containing lactobacilli and bifidobacteria, which can be activated through liquid (such as water). They are part of our natural gut flora and are also available as nutritional supplements in capsule or powder form from drugstores or online retailers. As well as having a positive impact on our gastrointestinal tract, these compounds are ideal for fermenting nut milk products.

ROASTING

Nuts and seeds can be roasted gently to unlock their full flavor, a fabulous crunch, and plenty of umami.

The quickest method is to toast them in a small dry pan while you are cooking. It is important to keep the temperature fairly low, which will mean roasting the nuts or seeds for longer — and, of course, you need to keep tossing the contents of the pan. This prevents any dark or burned patches, which can easily happen if you get distracted by cooking other things at the same time.

A more energy-efficient approach is to roast batches of nuts and seeds for your pantry to give you a convenient supply for everyday use. Preheat the oven to 250–300°F (120–150°C) (convection setting) and bake several sheets with different nuts and seeds at the same time. Once again, it is important to toss the nuts and seeds regularly and keep a close eye on them, as they brown at different rates. Seeds need 12–15 minutes in the oven. Macadamias, Brazil nuts, and walnuts require 15–20 minutes, while cashews, almonds, hazelnuts, and peanuts may need as long as 20–25 minutes. You can also toast coconut flakes and chips this way; they will be golden brown after about 10 minutes. When the nuts or seeds are shimmering and golden brown, remove them from the oven and let cool completely at room temperature. Finally, they can be transferred to separate storage jars to be enjoyed whenever required.

Personally, I always double up my baking sheets, for example putting macadamia nuts on one half and Brazil nuts on the other. A second sheet can hold almonds and hazelnuts. And finally, I slide a casserole dish with some mixed seeds into the oven.

What's the point of roasting?

Cashews acquire their distinctive characteristics when roasted to a golden color. They become crunchier and their flavor is enhanced.

Peanuts and *pistachios* are most popular when roasted and salted rather than plain.

Hazelnuts develop their typical intense flavor through roasting, which also makes it easier to remove their thin papery skin.

Almonds develop a mild and slightly sweet taste.

Brazil nuts become more buttery.

Macadamias develop a nuttier flavor.

Sunflower seeds, pumpkin seeds, and *sesame seeds* become crunchier when roasted and taste even better when scattered over salads and vegetables.

Walnuts lose their bitter note and develop more umami.

Coconut chips and *flakes* acquire a rounded nutty flavor when roasted and introduce a Caribbean fragrance to your kitchen.

CHOPPING

Chopping, grinding, or blending nuts and seeds is very easy to do at home with the right kitchen equipment. Nuts and other plant seeds (including grains and pulses) oxidize more quickly when chopped or ground due to the larger surface area, which is why I prefer to buy whole nuts. Then I can decide for myself whether I want roughly chopped seeds in a salad or curry or whether I might leave them whole when baking bread. Or, perhaps I might grind them finely using a food processor if I'm cooking nutty rissoles (recipe see p. 210) or if they are going to be used for a cake.

To chop nuts, all you need are a board and a large knife. A powerful food processor, free-standing blender, or an immersion blender with an S-blade can be used to roughly chop nuts. If you want a finely ground consistency or if you are making nut butter, you will ideally need a very powerful blender. But don't worry if you only have a small kitchen or don't want to be surrounded by lots of equipment. All the recipes in this book can easily be made by purchasing ready ground nuts or nut butter. Alternatively, chopping everything using a knife and board also works fine.

MAKING NUT BUTTER

If you want to make your own nut or seed butter, first you need to roast the nuts or seeds. Roasting transforms the color from pale to golden and triggers a structural change that allows the fats to be extracted more quickly and the butter to bind more easily when the nuts are processed. After roasting, it's important to allow the nuts or seeds to cool completely before processing, so the butter doesn't clump.

As soon as the nuts are cool, they should be chopped in a powerful blender using the lowest setting and then finely ground until the mixture begins to hold together. At this stage, the fats are emerging, and the mixture will gradually become creamier. Ideally, leave the blender running on high for a while and push the mixture down every so often using a spoon or other implement. Keep a close eye on the consistency to make sure you end up with the desired texture. If you like your nut or seed butter crunchy and with a bit of texture, stop the blending process at the relevant point. During the final minutes in the blender, the nut or seed butter can be flavored with sea salt, vanilla powder, or other spices.

The fats that are released from nuts and seeds form a protective layer on the surface, which means the butter will stay fresh for a long time. The oily layer inhibits oxidation and prevents bacteria from getting in. Consequently, nut and seed butters have a shelf life of several months, and if well chilled, they can even last for years.

The best homemade nut butters are those using **almonds**, **hazelnuts**, **macadamias**, or a blend of **Brazil nuts**, **cashews**, and **almonds**. Delicious results can also be achieved with **walnuts**. For processing nuts and seeds with a lower fat content and a higher proportion of protein or skin, including peanuts, cashews, and seeds, you will generally need more professional equipment, such as a colloid mill or a stone grinder, to produce a fine, creamy texture. For this reason, using shop-bought products is recommended here.

Due to the altered fat structure in nut butter, it is particularly useful as a substitute for highly processed oils when making sauces, marinades, dressings, mousses, and custards. Creamy salad dressings and marinades can be created without any additional oil, and you can rustle up spreads and mayonnaise without pure fat. As well as tasting great, these recipes are easier to digest and, if eaten in moderation, are good for the waistline. This is because nuts keep you feeling full for longer and supply all the important substances required for the body to efficiently metabolize the fats they contain.

BASIC RECIPES FOR NUT MILKS AND NUT MILK PRODUCTS

From left to right: Nut Parmesan, mozzarella with psyllium husks, mozzarella with tapioca starch (bottom), cashew cream cheese (top), cashew quark, cashew yogurt, nut milk

The ideal nuts for making nut milk are almonds, hazelnuts, and cashews. For nut quark, yogurt, and cream cheese, cashews are particularly good, because they have the most neutral flavor. If you want to make your own nut ricotta, you can't go wrong with almonds or a combination of cashews and macadamias. If you want to have a go at making cheese using raw ingredients in the style of Camembert or similar cheeses, cashews are the recommended option.

Due to their texture and intense flavor, walnuts, pecans, Brazil nuts, and tiger nuts are only suitable to a limited extent for making milk, quark, and so on.

ALMOND, HAZELNUT, AND CASHEW MILK

MAKES 1 LARGE BOTTLE

Preparation time
15–20 minutes + overnight soaking

Kitchen equipment
Freestanding or immersion blender, nut milk bag

Ingredients
· 3 ½ ounces (100 g) almonds, hazelnuts, or cashew pieces (or whole cashews), soaked in water overnight
· 1 pinch salt
· optional: 2 tbsp maple syrup (or 2–3 pitted dates, soaked in water overnight)

Drain the nuts in a sieve and rinse with cold water. Blend the nuts with 1 cup (240 ml) of water on the lowest setting, then at full power until finely ground. Add an additional 1 cup (240 ml) of water, the salt, and the maple syrup, if using, and process again for 30–60 seconds.

Cashew milk can be used immediately, as it contains no components that need to be filtered. Almond and hazelnut milk require filter-ing before consumption. Pour the nut milk into a nut milk bag over a large bowl. Seal the bag at the top and squeeze it out vigorously over the bowl until all that remains in the bag is the dry pulp. Decant the nut milk into a clean bottle. It will keep for about 5 days in the refrigerator.

Quick and easy: Nut milk in 3 minutes
Here is a quick way to make nut milk — perfect for your morning coffee or cereal — that takes just a few minutes. Blend 1–2 tsp of nut butter with ⅓–¾ cup (80–180 ml) of warm water and use immediately.

Nut milk bag
A nut milk bag is a bag-shaped straining cloth used to filter plant-based milks. The fine mesh of the hemp or linen fabric allows liquid to pass through while any fibrous materials are held back, making it easy to separate the nut milk from the pulp. Nut milk bags are available in zero waste stores or from online retailers. A fine laundry net, which can be found in drugstores, is a cheaper alternative, though the material is not particularly high quality.

CASHEW QUARK, YOGURT, AND CREAM CHEESE

MAKES ABOUT 1 POUND (450 G) OF QUARK OR CREAM CHEESE OR 2 ¼ POUNDS (1 KG) YOGURT

Preparation time
15 minutes + overnight soaking + 8–12 hours fermentation time

Kitchen equipment
Freestanding or immersion blender

For the basic mixture
· 14 ounces (400 g) cashew pieces (or whole cashews; alternatively 9 ounces (250 g) cashews and 5 ¼ ounces (150 g) macadamias or almonds for a more rounded flavor and a grainier consistency), soaked in water overnight
· 1 tsp probiotic powder (such as OMNi-BiOTiC®, VSL#3®, or a different probiotic powder or capsule, available at drugstores)

For the quark
· zest and juice of ½ lemon
· 1 pinch salt

For the cream cheese
· 2–3 tbsp light miso (shiro miso or lupin miso)

Drain the cashews in a sieve and rinse with cold water. Purée the nuts with ¾–1 ¼ cups (180–300 ml) of water, stirring as needed to loosen the mixture, until thick and creamy. Add the probiotic powder and mix well. For the **quark continue** from **(1)**, for the **yogurt** from **(2)**, and for the **cream cheese** from **(3)**.

(1) For the quark, transfer the mixture to a large, clean jar, cover loosely, and leave to ferment for 8–12 hours at room temperature. As soon as the mixture smells slightly sour and little bubbles are visible, seal the jar and refrigerate to halt the fermentation. Before using the quark (such as in desserts, or for mozzarella or dips) adjust the flavor with lemon zest, lemon juice, and salt. Use the quark within 4–5 days.

(2) For the yogurt, stir an additional 1 ⅔–2 cups (400–480 ml) of water into the mixture to achieve the desired consistency. Transfer the mixture to a large, clean jar, cover loosely, and leave to ferment for 8–12 hours at room temperature. As soon as the mixture smells slightly sour and little bubbles are visible, seal the jar and refrigerate to halt the fermentation. Use the yogurt within 4–5 days.

(3) For the cream cheese, stir the miso into the mixture — miso supplies additional probiotic cultures and produces a lovely cheesy flavor. Transfer the mixture to a large, clean jar, cover loosely, and leave to ferment for 8–12 hours at room temperature. As soon as the mixture smells slightly sour and little bubbles are visible, seal the jar and refrigerate to halt the fermentation. Use the cream cheese within 4–5 days.

Tip:

To make a particularly delicious cream cheese, adjust the flavor by adding additional ingredients after fermentation. For 3 ½ ounces (100 g) of cream cheese, stir in 1 tsp of lemon zest, some lemon juice, 1 heaping tsp of yeast flakes, and some salt.

Did you know:

Probiotics vary in terms of their potency. That is why it is best to experiment a bit to figure out how much is needed. If nothing is happening after 8 hours, you need a couple of grams extra, if the mixture is working after 4 hours in the kitchen, you will need to rein in the quantities slightly.

Also: Fermented yogurt can be used as a "starter" for a new mixture. Just stir 1 tbsp of the yogurt into the basic mixture — there is no need to add a probiotic).

ALMOND RICOTTA

MAKES ABOUT 1 POUND (450 G) RICOTTA

Preparation time
15 minutes + overnight soaking + 8–12 hours
fermentation time

Kitchen equipment
Freestanding or immersion blender, nut milk bag

Ingredients
· 9 ounces (250 g) almonds (or 5 ¼ ounces (150 g)
  almonds and 3 ½ ounces (100 g) macadamia nuts),
  soaked in water overnight
· 2 tbsp lemon juice
· 1–2 tbsp light miso (shiro miso or lupin miso)
· ½ tsp probiotic powder (such as OMNi-BiOTiC®,
  VSL#3®, or a different probiotic powder or
  capsule, available at drugstores)
· 1 pinch ground nutmeg
· 1 pinch cayenne pepper
· salt

Drain the almonds in a sieve and rinse with
cold water. Blend the nuts with enough water
to almost cover them until thick and creamy.
Add the lemon juice, miso, probiotic powder,
nutmeg, and cayenne pepper and mix well.
Season lightly with salt.

Transfer the mixture to a nut milk bag and
place in a sieve suspended over a bowl. Leave
to mature and drain for 8–12 hours at room
temperature. Put the ricotta mixture in a
large, clean jar, refrigerate, and use within 4–5
days.

MOZZARELLA WITH PSYLLIUM HUSKS

MAKES 6–8 LITTLE BALLS

Preparation time
15 minutes + 8 hours chilling time (+ 15 minutes +
overnight soaking + 8–12 hours fermentation for
the cashew quark)

Kitchen equipment
Freestanding or immersion blender

Ingredients
· 1 ounce (30 g) ground psyllium husks
· 1 tbsp shiro miso
· 1 tbsp lemon juice
· 2 tsp salt
· 9 ounces (250 g) cashew quark
  (basic recipe see p. 25)

Briefly purée 1 ⅔ cups (400 ml) of water
with the psyllium husks, miso, lemon juice,
and salt. Add the cashew quark and mix in
quickly — the mixture will soon become stiff.
As soon as everything is well combined, divide the mixture between 6–8 small, clean
jars, cover loosely, and refrigerate for 8 hours
to allow the psyllium husks to swell and the
mozzarella to become firmer. Remove the
mozzarella balls from the jars and cut into
slices. They will keep for 4–5 days in a well-
sealed container in the refrigerator.

MOZZARELLA WITH TAPIOCA STARCH

MAKES 8–12 LITTLE BALLS

Preparation time
45 minutes + overnight soaking + 24 hours fermentation + 20 minutes chilling time

Kitchen equipment
Freestanding or immersion blender

Ingredients
· 5 ¼ ounces (150 g) cashew pieces (or whole cashews), soaked in water overnight
· 10 ounces (300 g) silken tofu (or soy yogurt)
· 5 ½ tsp salt
· 1 tsp probiotic powder (such as OMNi-BiOTiC®, VSL#3®, or a different probiotic powder or capsule, available at drugstores)
· 1–2 tbsp light miso (shiro miso or lupin miso)
· 3 tbsp tapioca flour
· 2 tbsp lemon juice
· ¼ ounce (7.5 g) agar-agar

Drain the cashews in a sieve and rinse with cold water. Purée the nuts with the silken tofu, 1 ½ teaspoons of the salt, the probiotic powder, miso, and ⅓ cup plus 2 tablespoons (100 ml) of water until smooth and creamy. Transfer to a large, clean jar, place the lid loosely on top, and leave to ferment for about 24 hours at room temperature.

Put the fermented mixture in a large bowl and stir in the tapioca flour and lemon juice. Stir the agar-agar into ½ cup (120 ml) of water in a large saucepan and bring to a boil. Reduce the heat to moderate and simmer for 2–3 minutes. Add the fermented mixture and simmer, stirring constantly, for another 6–8 minutes. The mixture will soon stiffen, so it is vital to keep stirring vigorously to prevent it catching (don't worry if it sticks slightly to the bottom of the saucepan). Remove from the heat and immediately fill a large bowl with ice cubes and about 8 ½ cups (2 liters) of water. Use an ice-cream scoop or two large spoons to create 8–12 little balls from the mozzarella mixture

and immerse in the ice water for 20 minutes. Meanwhile, stir the remaining 4 tsp of salt into 2 cups (480 ml) of water in a large container. Transfer the chilled mozzarella balls to a large, clean jar and pour in the brine. They will keep for about 1 week in a well-sealed container in the refrigerator.

NUT PARMESAN

MAKES 1 SMALL JAR

Preparation time
10 minutes + 15–20 minutes baking + cooling time

Kitchen equipment
Food processor or spice grinder

Ingredients
· 3 ½ ounces (100 g) each of cashew pieces (or whole cashews) and Brazil nuts (or 7 ounces (200 g) cashews)
· 1–2 tbsp nutritional yeast flakes
· 1 pinch ground turmeric
· 1 pinch cayenne pepper
· 1 pinch salt
· freshly ground pepper

Preheat the oven to 250–300°F (120–150°C) (convection setting). Spread the nuts on a baking sheet and roast for 15–20 minutes until golden. Let cool completely.

Grind the nuts with the yeast flakes, turmeric, cayenne pepper, salt, and pepper until crumbly. Adjust the seasoning if necessary, then transfer to a large jar with a lid. The Parmesan will keep for 10–14 days in the refrigerator.

BASIC RECIPES FOR DRESSINGS, MARINADES, AND SAUCES

Salad dressing with nut butter (top left), peanut and orange sauce (center left), cashew hollandaise (bottom left), cashew béchamel (top right), lemony sauce with tahini (center right)

SALAD DRESSING WITH NUT BUTTER

MAKES 1 LARGE JAR

Preparation time: 5 minutes

Kitchen equipment: Freestanding or immersion blender

Ingredients

· ½ cup (120 ml) apple cider vinegar (or white balsamic vinegar or white wine vinegar)
· ¾ cup (180 ml) apple juice (or water)
· ½ cup (100 g) nut butter of your choice
· 1 tbsp maple syrup (or agave syrup)
· 1 tsp mustard
· 1 generous pinch salt
· optional: 1 tsp dried (or freshly chopped) herbs, chopped garlic, miso, lemon zest, and/or a few fresh berries, depending which salad is being made

Purée the apple cider vinegar, apple juice, nut butter, maple syrup, mustard, salt, and optional ingredients, if using, until creamy. The dressing will keep for 4–5 days in a clean, well-sealed jar in the refrigerator.

LEMONY SAUCE WITH TAHINI

MAKES 1 LARGE JAR

Preparation time: 5 minutes

Kitchen equipment: Freestanding or immersion blender

Ingredients

· ⅓ cup plus 2 tbsp (100 ml) lemon juice
· ⅔ cup (160 g) light tahini (or blanched almond butter)
· 1 pinch salt
· optional: ground cumin, curry powder, ground turmeric, and/or lemon zest

Purée the lemon juice, tahini, salt, and spices, if using, with 1 cup (240 ml) of water. The sauce will keep for 4–5 days in a clean, well-sealed jar in the refrigerator. It tastes fabulous with hummus, roasted vegetables, tabbouleh, or salads made from other grains.

CASHEW HOLLANDAISE

MAKES ABOUT 4 ¼ CUPS (1 LITER)

Preparation time: 20 minutes

Kitchen equipment: Freestanding or immersion blender

Ingredients

· 5 ¼ ounces (150 g) canned or jarred white beans (drained weight)
· ¾ cup (150 g) cashew butter
· ⅓ cup (20 g) nutritional yeast flakes
· zest of ½ lemon
· 2 tbsp lemon juice
· 2 tbsp white wine vinegar
· ½ tsp kala namak (Himalayan black salt, available from health food stores or online retailers)
· 1 pinch ground turmeric
· salt
· 1 ounce (30 g) cornstarch
· 4 to 8 tbsp (60–120 ml) sparkling dry white wine
· ground white pepper

Put the beans in a sieve and rinse with cold water. Purée the beans with the cashew butter, yeast flakes, lemon zest and juice, white wine vinegar, kala namak, turmeric, 1 tsp of salt, and 2 cups (480 ml) of water until creamy.

Heat this creamy mixture in a large saucepan, stirring constantly, until simmering. Combine the cornstarch with about 5 tbsp of water in a small bowl until smooth. As soon as the mixture in the saucepan is simmering, add the cornstarch paste and the white wine and bring to a boil. Reduce the heat to moderate and cook, stirring, until thick. Adjust the flavor with additional white wine, salt, and pepper.

Tip:

The hollandaise sauce will keep in a clean, well-sealed container in the refrigerator for 3–4 days and can be served with asparagus (recipe see p. 69) or as a dip for potatoes or roasted vegetables.

CASHEW BÉCHAMEL

MAKES ABOUT 4 ¼ CUPS (1 LITER)
Preparation time: 20 minutes
Kitchen equipment: Freestanding or immersion blender

Ingredients
· 5 ¼ ounces (150 g) canned or jarred white beans (drained weight)
· ¾ cup (150 g) cashew butter
· ¾ cup (45 g) nutritional yeast flakes
· 3 tbsp light miso (shiro miso or lupin miso)
· 2–3 tbsp white wine vinegar
· 1 pinch ground nutmeg
· salt
· 2 ½ tbsp tapioca flour (or cornstarch. However, the latter thickens slightly differently and will not produce the classic strands you get in a béchamel sauce)
· ground white pepper

Put the beans in a sieve and rinse with cold water. Purée the beans with the cashew butter, yeast flakes, miso, white wine vinegar, nutmeg, 1 level tsp of salt, and 2 ½ cups (600 ml) of warm water.

Heat the mixture in a large saucepan, stirring constantly, until simmering. Combine the tapioca flour with about 5 tbsp of water in a small bowl until smooth. As soon as the mixture in the saucepan is simmering, add the tapioca paste and bring to a boil. Reduce the heat to moderate and cook, stirring, until the mixture thickens. Season with salt and pepper.

Tip:

Making béchamel in advance? You would only do that to save time if you were making lasagna the next day, right? Wrong! Once you realize this béchamel sauce can also be poured over a gratin, or used as a substitute for crème fraîche with pan-fried vegetables, or just eaten as a dip on its own, you will want to make sure you always have some in your fridge. It will keep for 4–5 days in a clean, well-sealed jar.

Quick and easy: Mac-no-cheese sauce

The basic cashew béchamel recipe can easily be adapted to make a tasty mac-no-cheese sauce. Peel and roughly chop 1 onion and 2 cloves of garlic and fry both in some olive oil until golden. When puréeing the basic mixture, add the onion and garlic, plus 1 tsp each of curry powder, smoked paprika, and liquid smoke, if using, then continue making the sauce as described. Serve with macaroni.

PEANUT AND ORANGE SAUCE

MAKES 1 LARGE JAR
Preparation time: 20 minutes
Kitchen equipment: Freestanding or immersion blender

Ingredients
· 1 piece ginger, roughly 1 inch (2.5 cm)
· 1 mild fresh chile
· 2 ¾ ounces (80 g) salted roasted peanuts
· ½ cup (100 g) peanut butter
· ⅓ cup (80 ml) tamari soy sauce (strong, dark soy sauce)
· zest of 1 orange
· ¾ cup (180 ml) orange juice
· 2–3 tbsp agave syrup (or rice syrup)
· 1 tsp chile flakes
· optional: rice vinegar

Finely chop the ginger and slice the chile, removing the seeds if preferred. Roughly chop the peanuts.

Purée the peanut butter, tamari, orange zest and juice, agave syrup, and chile flakes. Fold in the ginger, chile, and peanuts. Season with some rice vinegar, if using.

Tip:

The sauce will keep for 4–5 days in the refrigerator in a clean, well-sealed jar and tastes delicious with roasted asparagus (recipe see p. 65) or stir-fried vegetables.

SPRING

Fields glisten with morning frost and dewdrops, as the natural world awakens and tentatively stretches up towards the sun. A trip to the market offers the enticing prospect of fresh greens and wild herbs. Everything is sprouting and growing. What we crave are raw delicacies packed with vitamins and flavor, allowing us to savor their slightly bitter notes and rich green leaves.

OMEGA-3 PORRIDGE WITH RHUBARB COMPOTE

WALNUT · HEMP · FLAXSEED OIL

First make some hemp seed milk. Blend the hemp seeds with 1 ⅔ cups (400 ml) of warm water for 1 minute. There is no need to strain the milk through a cloth, as the hemp seed fibers will not be noticeable in the porridge.

Roughly chop the walnuts and combine in a bowl with the oats, flaxseed meal, berries, and salt. Pour over the warm milk and leave to swell briefly.

Meanwhile, prepare the rhubarb compote. Trim and peel the rhubarb then chop into small pieces. Quarter, core, and finely chop the apple. Heat some coconut oil in a small saucepan and sauté the diced apple over moderate heat until golden on all sides. Add the white cane sugar and vanilla powder and allow to caramelize slightly. Add the chopped rhubarb with about 2 tablespoons of water and simmer gently with the lid on until the rhubarb begins to fall apart.

Stir the porridge well using a balloon whisk to ensure a creamy consistency before serving. Divide between four large glasses, drizzle each with 1 tablespoon of flaxseed oil and 1 tablespoon of maple syrup and serve with the rhubarb compote.

SERVES 4

Preparation time
25 minutes

Kitchen equipment
Freestanding or immersion blender

For the porridge
· 4 tbsp hulled hemp seeds
· 2 ounces (60 g) walnuts
· 1 ¼ cups (110 g) (gluten-free) oats
· 2 tbsp flaxseed meal
· 4 tbsp dried berries (or other dried fruit)
· 1 pinch salt

For the rhubarb compote
· 4 large rhubarb stalks
· 1 small apple
· coconut oil (or vegan margarine)
· 1–2 tbsp white cane sugar
· 1 pinch bourbon vanilla powder

Also
· 4 tbsp flaxseed oil
· 4 tbsp maple syrup

SOFT OAT AND MILLET BREAD

BUCKWHEAT · BRAZIL NUT

MAKES 1 LOAF

Preparation time

20 minutes + 45 minutes rising time + 1 hour baking time

Kitchen equipment

Hand mixer or stand mixer, approx. 12 × 4-inch (30 × 10 cm) loaf pan

Ingredients

· 3 cups (240 g) (gluten-free) oats
· ¾ cup (100 g) millet flour (or ragi flour)
· ¾ cup (100 g) whole-grain buckwheat flour (or spelt flour)
· ¾ cup (80 g) flaxseed meal
· 4 tbsp ground psyllium husks
· 1 tbsp salt
· optional: 1 tbsp bread spice
· ¾ ounce (20 g) fresh yeast
· 3 ½ ounces (100 g) Brazil nuts
· optional: olive oil

In a large bowl, combine the oats, millet flour, buckwheat flour, flaxseed meal, psyllium husks, salt, and bread spice, if using.

Pour 2 ½ cups (600 ml) of lukewarm water into a medium container, crumble in the yeast, and stir to dissolve. Add this mixture to the dry ingredients and knead using the dough hook attachment for at least 5 minutes until you have a smooth and elastic dough. Roughly chop the Brazil nuts and work these into the dough.

Line the loaf pan with parchment paper, leaving a 1-inch (2.5 cm) overhang on the long sides. Transfer the bread dough to the pan, moisten the surface slightly with water, and smooth it out. Cover the pan with a kitchen towel and let rise in a warm place for 45 minutes. About 10 minutes before the end of the rising time, preheat the oven to 425°F (220°C) (convection setting). Pour roughly 2 cups (480 ml) of water into a second ovenproof dish.

Brush the top of the risen dough with olive oil, if using. Slide the loaf pan into the oven and place the dish filled with water on the rack underneath, working quickly to ensure as little heat as possible escapes. Bake the bread for 5 minutes then reduce the heat to 350°F (180°C) and continue baking for another 45 minutes. Carefully lift the bread out of the pan using the parchment paper, set directly on the oven rack, and bake for another 10 minutes to create a crust all over. Remove the bread from the oven and let cool completely on a wire rack before slicing.

Quick and easy: bread spice

Bread spice, which gives German breads their richness and warmth, is easily found at German supermarkets and some online retailers, but you can also whip up your own. Simply combine ground fennel, coriander, caraway, and aniseeds in equal parts and store in an airtight container for use in all your homemade loaves.

POTATO AND WILD GARLIC SPREAD

CASHEW · NUTMEG

SERVES 4 TO 6

Preparation time
20 minutes + 30–35 minutes
cooking time

Ingredients
· 14 ounces (400 g) starchy potatoes
· salt
· 1 ¾ ounces (50 g) cashews
· 3 ½ ounces (100 g) wild garlic (or
  chives)
· ¼ cup (50 g) cashew butter
· 2 tbsp white balsamic vinegar (or
  mild white wine vinegar)
· 1 pinch ground nutmeg
· freshly ground pepper

Recipe photo see p. 39

Put the potatoes in a medium saucepan with some salt, add just enough water to cover the potatoes, and cook with the lid on over moderate heat for 30–35 minutes until soft. Drain in a sieve and let the potatoes cool.

Meanwhile, chop the cashews and toast in a small dry pan over moderate heat until golden brown. Finely chop the wild garlic. Peel the slightly cooled potatoes, transfer to a bowl, and mash with a fork or potato masher.

Mix the cashew butter, white balsamic vinegar, nutmeg, and some salt with the potatoes. Fold in the wild garlic and use a fork to stir the spread until smooth. Season with salt and pepper and serve sprinkled with the roasted cashews.

Tip:

If covered, the spread will keep in the refrigerator for 4–5 days and tastes fantastic either on bread or served as a dip with vegetables.

GREEN TOFU AND HEMP PÂTÉ

ARUGULA · PARSLEY · WALNUT · TAMARI

Roughly chop the arugula and parsley. Roughly chop the walnuts and crumble the tofu. Zest and juice the lemons.

Blend the arugula, parsley, walnuts, tofu, lemon zest, half the lemon juice, hemp seeds, tamari, olive oil, maple syrup, and paprika, pulsing until everything is well combined but stopping before the consistency is completely smooth. Season with salt, pepper, and possibly more lemon juice.

Tip:

If covered, the spread will keep in the refrigerator for 4–5 days and tastes fantastic either on bread or served as a dip with potatoes or roasted vegetables.

SERVES 4 TO 8

Preparation time
20 minutes

Kitchen equipment
Freestanding or immersion blender

Ingredients
· 1 handful arugula leaves
· 1 bunch fresh parsley
· 1 ¾ ounces (50 g) walnuts
· 7 ounces (200 g) natural tofu (or smoked tofu for a heartier flavor)
· 2 lemons
· ⅓ cup (50 g) hulled hemp seeds
· 6 tbsp tamari soy sauce (strong, dark soy sauce)
· 4 tbsp olive oil
· 2 tbsp maple syrup
· 1 tsp smoked paprika (such as Pimentón de la Vera; alternatively, hot or sweet paprika)
· salt
· freshly ground pepper

Recipe photo see p. 39

THE
WALNUT

Walnuts are arguably the classic nut and were long thought to be a type of stone fruit in botanical terms. But it is now clear that walnuts are indeed nuts.

Walnut trees are leafy, deciduous members of the Juglandaceae family. The walnut tree is monoecious, which means it has both male and female flowers. The male flower heads mature roughly four weeks before the female flowers, and pollination is done by wind.

Walnut kernels are generally divided into two symmetrical halves, which are surrounded by a hard shell. The shell also consists of two halves, joined together by a bulging seam. The nut is enclosed inside a thick, green fruity layer, which gradually decays over time and splits open once the nut is edible.

In central Europe, walnuts are harvested in September and October. In California, harvesting takes place between August and November. It can sometimes take 10 to 15 years for a walnut tree to flower and bear fruit for the first time. To harvest the nuts, the walnuts are shaken from the trees, swept up, and soaked. During the machine cleaning process, the nuts are separated from the outer shell, washed, and then carefully dried for as long as necessary to ensure no mold develops.

HEALTH BENEFITS

Walnuts supply up to 62 percent fat (including lots of unsaturated fatty acids), roughly 15 percent protein, and roughly 11 percent carbohydrate. They are particularly recommended because they are the nut with the highest linolenic acid content (Omega-3 fatty acid) and have an abundance of tocopherols (vitamin E derivatives). Like many other nuts, walnuts contain plenty of B vitamins, minerals, and trace elements.

Regular walnut consumption can lower the risk of developing Type 2 diabetes. In combination with linseed oil, which is rich in Omega-3 fatty acids, walnuts can have a beneficial effect on the health of our blood vessels and offer protection against cardiovascular disease. The polyphenols contained in the nuts can scavenge free radicals and protect our cells against oxidative stress.

ECONOMIC CHALLENGES

Walnut trees are most commonly found in the Mediterranean, on the Balkan peninsula, in North America, the Near East, Central Asia, and China. Most of the walnuts sold on the global market come from China and the United States. Walnuts also thrive in central Europe, but are primarily cultivated for sale at local markets, rather than in supermarkets or health-food stores.

To buy products that are as sustainable and environmentally friendly as possible, it is important to look for organically cultivated goods and preferably nuts that are grown in your own country or that have been directly imported from neighboring countries.

CULINARY USES

Walnuts have a strong flavor with a hint of bitterness and a slightly sweet element. The sky really is the limit when it comes to their culinary uses. Roasted, salted walnuts add the perfect finishing touch to an autumn salad. A hearty loaf or aromatic herb pesto can also be greatly enhanced by the characteristic flavor of walnuts. Desserts and pastries are another ideal place to use walnuts. Caramelized walnuts offer a perfect balance between sweet and savory. They are an essential ingredient in Christmas baking, ensuring lebkuchen, cookies, and various other delicious treats are not too sweet.

Main cultivation areas for walnuts

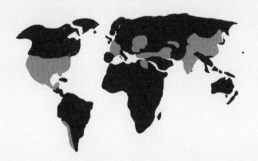

GOLDEN TURMERIC CREAM

CASHEW · VANILLA · CINNAMON

Heat the coconut oil in a small saucepan until melted.

Drain the cashews in a sieve and rinse with cold water. Thoroughly purée the coconut oil, drained cashews, agave syrup, rice milk, and ground spices, until you have a silky-smooth cream. Season with salt.

Tip:

This turmeric cream is ideal as a sandwich spread or as a topping for the carrot and banana bread (recipe see p. 48) or a warm porridge (recipe see p. 194). It will keep covered in the refrigerator for about 5 days.

Quick and easy: Sweet turmeric spice mix

It's always useful to have a spice mix in your larder! Just combine 2 tablespoons of ground turmeric, 1 tablespoon each ground cinnamon, ground cardamom, ground ginger, and bourbon vanilla powder, plus 5 tablespoons of raw cane sugar and store in an airtight jar. Bring 1 cup (240 ml) of plant-based milk to a boil and add 1 teaspoon of the spice mix for an exquisite, golden turmeric drink. This mix is also a fabulous way to spice up and dye Frozen Cubes (recipe see p. 138/139) or perfect for stirring into a warm bowl of porridge.

MAKES 1 MEDIUM JAR

Preparation time
10 minutes + overnight soaking

Kitchen equipment
Freestanding or immersion blender

Ingredients
· 3 tbsp coconut oil
· 5 ¼ ounces (150 g) cashew pieces (or whole cashews), soaked in water overnight
· 2 ¼ tbsp agave syrup
· ⅔ cup (150 ml) rice milk
· 1 pinch each ground turmeric, bourbon vanilla powder, ground nutmeg, ground cinnamon, ground allspice, and cayenne pepper (or 1 tsp pumpkin spice mix)
· salt

CARROT AND BANANA BREAD WITH GOLDEN TURMERIC CREAM

CASHEW · CINNAMON · CRISPY CARROT STRIPS

MAKES 1 LOAF

Preparation time
40 minutes + 45 minutes baking
+ cooling time

Kitchen equipment
Hand mixer or stand mixer,
approx. 12 × 4-inch (30 × 10 cm)
loaf pan

For the bread and crispy carrot strips
· 3 cups (250 g) (gluten-free) oat flour
· ¾ cup (100 g) whole-grain buckwheat flour
· ½ cup (52 g) flaxseed meal
· 1 tsp baking powder
· ½ tsp baking soda
· 1½ tsp ground cinnamon
· salt
· 3 ripe bananas
· 10 ounces (300 g) carrots
· ¼ cup (50 g) cashew butter
· 1 splash lemon juice (or a light vinegar)
· coconut oil

Also
· golden turmeric cream
(recipe see p. 47)

Preheat the oven to 350°F (180°C) (convection setting). In a large bowl, combine the oat flour, buckwheat flour, flaxseed meal, baking powder, baking soda, 1 teaspoon of the cinnamon, and a pinch of salt.

Peel the bananas and mash with a fork on a plate. Peel and grate the carrots, setting aside the strips of peel for later. In a small bowl, stir together the cashew butter, ⅓ cup (80 ml) of water, and the lemon juice. Add this mixture, along with the mashed bananas, to the dry ingredients and whisk until smooth and combined. Fold in the grated carrots. Line the loaf pan with parchment paper, leaving a 1-inch (2.5 cm) overhang on the long sides, pour in the batter, and smooth the surface.

To make the crispy carrot strips, melt some coconut oil in a small saucepan. Toss the reserved carrot peel strips, a pinch of salt, and the remaining cinnamon in the coconut oil. Line a baking sheet with parchment paper then arrange the carrot strips on top. Put the carrots and the bread in the oven and bake for 10 minutes. Turn the carrots and continue baking for another 5 minutes until crisp and dry. Remove the carrots from the oven and continue baking the bread for another 20 minutes until golden brown (an inserted skewer should come out clean — if any mixture sticks to it, extend the baking time slightly). Turn off the oven and leave the bread to continue baking for another 10 minutes. Remove the bread from the oven, carefully lift it out of the pan using the parchment paper, and let it cool completely on a wire rack.

Cover the carrot and banana bread with the turmeric cream and scatter over the crispy carrot strips. Enjoy for breakfast with a hot cup of tea or coffee.

VELVETY BEET AND CELERY SOUP

APPLE · HORSERADISH · SESAME SEED · SUNFLOWER SEED

SERVES 4

Preparation time
1 hour

Kitchen equipment
Freestanding or immersion blender

Recipe photo see p. 50/51

Cut off the root ends of the beets. If the skin is unblemished, it can be left on; otherwise, peel the beets. Pluck off a couple of leaves from the celery and set aside to use as decoration. Peel the potatoes, onion, and garlic. Finely chop the onion and garlic. Cut the beets, potatoes, and celery into large pieces.

Heat some olive oil in a large saucepan. Fry the onion, garlic, and cloves until fragrant and slightly browned. Add the beets, potatoes, and celery and sauté briskly over high heat, stirring constantly. Deglaze the pan with the apple juice, scraping any delicious bits from the bottom of the pan, and pour in the vegetable broth. Reduce the heat to low, cover the pan, and simmer for 20 minutes until the vegetables are tender.

Meanwhile, peel and finely grate the horseradish. Cut the apple into quarters and remove the core, then slice each quarter into thin matchsticks. Toast the sunflower seeds in a small dry pan over moderate heat then set aside.

Did you know:

The reason for using a blender here is not just to create a purée but also because breaking down the ingredients is the best way to release their distinctive flavors.

Blend the cooked vegetables until completely smooth. Add some salt and the tahini then process again. If the soup is too thick, stir in some hot water. Season with salt, vinegar, and possibly some more tahini.

Divide the soup between four deep bowls and garnish with the grated horseradish, apple matchsticks, sunflower seeds, and celery leaves. Serve immediately.

Ingredients
· 1 ¼ pounds (600 g) beets
· 2 celery stalks with leaves
· 2 small potatoes
· 1 onion
· 1 garlic clove
· olive oil
· 4 cloves
· 1 ⅔ cups (400 ml) apple juice
· 2 cups (480 ml) vegetable broth
· 1 piece horseradish, roughly ¾ inch (2 cm)
· 1 apple
· 4–6 tbsp sunflower seeds
· salt
· 2 tbsp light tahini (or a pale nut butter)
· 1–2 tbsp vinegar (or soy sauce)

Tastes great with:
Hearty whole-grain bread.

DOUBLE RADISH WITH GREEN POLENTA

PISTACHIO · APRICOT · LEMON

SERVES 4

Preparation time
1 hour

Kitchen equipment
Freestanding or immersion blender

For the polenta
· 1 ⅔ cups (400 ml) vegetable broth
· ½ tsp salt
· 1 ¼ cups (200 g) coarse polenta

For the pesto
· 1 lemon
· 2 bunches radishes with leaves
· 4 tbsp olive oil
· 1–2 tbsp mirin (sweet rice wine)

Also
· 2–4 garlic cloves
· 4–8 dried apricots
· 1 ¾ ounces (50 g) shelled pistachios
· olive oil (or canola oil)
· 2–3 tbsp apple syrup (or maple syrup)
· salt
· freshly ground pepper

To make the polenta, bring the vegetable broth and salt to a boil in a medium saucepan. Pour in the polenta, stirring constantly, and return to a boil. Turn off the heat, cover the pan, and leave to thicken for about 15 minutes.

Meanwhile, prepare the pesto. Zest and juice the lemon. Separate the leaves from the radishes and reserve a third of the leaves for later. Purée the remaining leaves with the lemon zest and juice, the olive oil, mirin, and ¾ cup (180 ml) of water to create a fine paste. Stir into the thickened polenta.

Slice the radishes in half. Peel the garlic cloves and crush using the flat side of a knife. Slice the apricots into strips. Roughly chop the pistachios.

Heat some olive oil in a pan. Sauté the garlic over moderate heat until fragrant. Place the radishes, cut side down, in the hot oil and sauté briskly over high heat until slightly browned. Add the apricots and the reserved radish leaves and continue frying briefly. Deglaze the pan with the apple syrup, scraping any delicious bits from the bottom of the pan, then season with salt and pepper. As soon as the leaves have wilted, remove the pan from the heat. Divide the polenta and radishes between plates and scatter with pistachios before serving.

RAW MISO KOHLRABI WITH STRAWBERRIES

MACADAMIA · MISO · THYME

Remove and discard the outer leaves from the kohlrabi. Slice the attractive inner leaves into thin strips. Peel the kohlrabi bulbs and cut into thin matchsticks. Put the kohlrabi leaves and matchsticks in a medium bowl and lightly season with salt. Hull the strawberries then cut into quarters or eighths. Strip the thyme leaves from the stems. Add the strawberries and thyme leaves to the kohlrabi.

For the dressing, stir together the macadamia nut butter, raspberry vinegar, agave syrup, sweet mustard, miso, and 5 tablespoons of water in a small bowl until creamy. Season with salt and pepper. Drizzle the dressing over the kohlrabi and strawberries, toss everything carefully, and divide between plates.

Roughly chop the macadamia nuts. Sprinkle each portion of salad with macadamias and scatter with wild herbs if using.

SERVES 4

Preparation time
30 minutes

For the salad
· 2 kohlrabi bulbs with leaves
· salt
· 9 ounces (250 g) strawberries
· 2–3 sprigs fresh thyme

For the dressing
· ¼ cup (50 g) macadamia nut butter (or another pale nut butter)
· 5 tbsp raspberry vinegar (or another fruity vinegar)
· 2 tbsp agave syrup
· 1 tsp Bavarian sweet mustard
· 1 tsp light miso (shiro miso or lupin miso)
· salt
· ground white pepper

Also
· ¾ cup (100 g) roasted macadamia nuts
· optional: edible wild herbs to decorate

Tastes great with:
Freshly baked baguette or ciabatta.

SUMMER ROLLS WITH A SPRING FEEL

RADISH · FERMENTED TOFU · ORANGE · PEANUT

**SERVES 4
(ROUGHLY 12–16 ROLLS)**

Preparation time
40 minutes

For the dip
· 1 orange
· ½ cup (100 g) peanut butter
· 3 tbsp tamari soy sauce (strong, dark soy sauce)
· 3 tbsp rice vinegar
· 2 tbsp maple syrup
· 1 fresh chile
· optional: 1 scallion
· 3 ½ ounces (100 g) salted roasted peanuts

For the summer rolls
· 3 ½ ounces (100 g) mixed fresh herbs and salad leaves (such as Thai basil, mizuna, loose leaf lettuce, arugula, and dandelion greens)
· 1 small bunch fresh cilantro
· 1 small bunch fresh mint
· 1 large carrot
· 6 button mushrooms
· 8 radishes with leaves
· 7 ounces (200 g) fermented tofu (available from Asian supermarkets of health food stores; or vegan feta)
· rice paper sheets

Zest and juice the orange for the dip. Stir both together with the peanut butter, tamari, rice vinegar, and maple syrup in a small bowl.

Cut the chile lengthwise in half, removing the seeds if preferred, and slice thinly. If using, clean the scallion if necessary and slice into thin rings. Roughly chop the peanuts. Stir the chile, scallion, and peanuts into the dip. Set aside to infuse.

Roughly chop the mixed herbs and salad leaves, along with the cilantro and mint, for the summer rolls. Cut the carrot into thin strips using a peeler. Clean the mushrooms then slice thinly. Separate the best leaves from the radishes and add to the herbs and salad leaves. Thinly slice the radishes. Slice the fermented tofu diagonally into thin strips.

Fill a large, shallow bowl with warm water. Briefly immerse a sheet of rice paper in the water, then spread it out on a large plate. Arrange slices of carrot, mushroom, and radish in a fan pattern in the center as desired. Top with a slice of fermented tofu and a few herbs and salad leaves. Fold the sides of the rice paper over the filling, then roll it up starting from the bottom.

Prepare the remaining rolls in the same way and serve with the peanut and chile dip.

Quick and easy: Fresh spring side salad
Use the leftover herbs, lettuce, and vegetables to rustle up a quick side salad. The dressing for the mango and fennel salad makes a great simple vinaigrette (recipe see p. 104). If you have all the ingredients, that salad is also lovely served alongside the summer rolls with any leftover herbs, lettuce, and vegetable mixed in.

THE PEANUT

Peanuts are not actually nuts at all but a kind of legume.

The **peanut plant** belongs to the Papilionaceous family and is related to beans and peas. These herbaceous plants grow to a height of 32 inches (80 centimeters). After pollination, the stems extend downwards, pressing the young fruit into the earth before the peanut plant develops from the flower. This is how peanuts grow underground, even though they are not part of the roots or bulb. When they are harvested, they are pulled from the ground in clusters. Unlike other pulses, the shell on the fruit does not open when ripe which is why it's legitimate to describe peanuts as "nuts."

Each shell generally contains two peanuts, but some varieties contain as many as four. The **peanut** itself can be round and as small as a pea, or oval and as large as a bean. Each nut consists of two halves, which are linked by the seedling. The peanut is enclosed in a reddish-brown skin that usually falls off after drying but will still be present on unshelled peanuts, which are more common at Christmas time — the skins can be easily rubbed off with your fingers.

HEALTH BENEFITS

Peanuts have a protein content of about 25 percent, the highest of any nut. They also have an impressive amino acid profile and contain lots of lysine, which is often lacking in plant-based diets. To ensure an optimal supply of protein, it is recommended that legumes are combined with grains (for example, bread with peanut butter or peanut curry with brown rice) to provide the perfect complement for the eight essential amino acids.

Peanuts offer plenty of other nutritional benefits too. They are one of the plant-based foods with the highest levels of magnesium and are a good source of potassium, calcium, zinc, copper, manganese, and iron, not to mention biotin, niacin, and vitamin E.

ECONOMIC CHALLENGES

Outside India and Argentina, the biggest peanut producers on the global market include the United States, Senegal, and Brazil. China is the largest producer in the world but uses the lion's share of its produce domestically.

To give peanuts a longer shelf life after harvesting, they must first be dried. In sustainable, fair trade cooperatives, peanuts are harvested by hand and dried in the sun to generate jobs and save energy. In conventional production, harvesting is automated, and the drying process takes place in industrial plants.

Organic, fair trade peanuts promote soil health in their country of origin and secure an adequate income for cooperatives. These production communities can decide collectively what to spend the generated revenue on — for instance, training sessions devoted to methods of cultivation and local processing.

CULINARY USES

Only after roasting do peanuts acquire their typical flavor, which is slightly earthy and sweet. They have all sorts of uses in cooking and baking and are a key ingredient in the regional cuisines of South East Asia, West Africa, and North America. Roasted, salted peanuts taste superb in Thai veggie stir-fries or spicy, fruity dips. Peanut butter adds a creamy texture to curries and sweet dishes. And who can resist the combination of peanut butter and banana on bread?

Main cultivation areas for peanuts

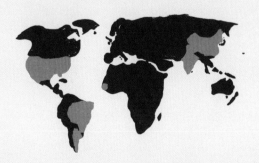

OVEN-BAKED ASPARAGUS WITH MANGO AND PEANUT SALSA

SCALLION · CHILE

For the salsa, clean the scallions if necessary and slice into thin rings. Thinly slice the chile, removing the seeds if preferred. Dice the dried mango. Stir together the mango purée, tamari, rice vinegar, peanut butter, and ume su in a medium bowl until smooth and combined. Fold in the scallions, chile, and dried mango and set aside to infuse.

Preheat the oven to 350°F (180°C) (convection setting). Remove the woody ends of the asparagus, peel the lower third of each spear if necessary, and arrange on a baking sheet. Drizzle with some peanut oil, lightly season with salt, and toss to coat. Bake for 20–25 minutes until tender.

Roughly chop the peanuts and the cilantro if using. Divide the asparagus between plates and scatter with peanuts and cilantro. Serve with the mango and peanut salsa.

Tastes great with:
Basmati or jasmine rice.

SERVES 4

Preparation time
30 minutes + 20–25 minutes cooking time

For the salsa
· 2 scallions
· 1 fresh chile
· 1 ¾ ounces (50 g) dried mango
· 3 ½ ounces (100 g) mango purée
· 5 tbsp tamari soy sauce (strong, dark soy sauce)
· 5 tbsp rice vinegar
· 2–3 tbsp crunchy peanut butter
· 2 tbsp ume su (sour umeboshi seasoning; available from Asian supermarkets or health food stores)

Also
· 2 ¼ pounds (1 kg) green asparagus
· peanut oil (or olive or canola oil)
· salt
· 1 ounce (30 g) salted roasted peanuts
· optional: 1 bunch fresh cilantro

ROASTED CARROTS WITH NUTTY QUINOA

ORANGE · CARROT GREENS · FENNEL SEED & HAZELNUT CRUNCH

SERVES 4

Preparation time
45 minutes

Ingredients
· 1 bunch baby carrots with greens
· vegetable oil
· 1 tsp ground cumin
· salt
· freshly ground pepper
· 1 tsp white cane sugar
· 1 cup (200 g) white quinoa
· 1 ¾ ounces (50 g) hazelnuts
· 1 tsp fennel seeds

For the marinade
· 1 orange
· 2 tbsp hazelnut butter
· 2 tbsp apple cider vinegar (or a
  mild white wine vinegar)
· 1 tsp mustard
· salt
· freshly ground pepper

Preheat the oven to 350°F (180°C) (convection setting). Line two baking sheets with parchment paper. Separate the carrots from the greens. Cut the carrots lengthwise in half and arrange, close together and cut side facing up, on one of the lined baking sheets. Very lightly brush with the vegetable oil, sprinkle with the cumin, and season with salt and pepper. Sprinkle the white cane sugar over the carrots so they caramelize slightly in the oven.

Put the carrot greens on the second lined baking sheet, drizzle with some vegetable oil, and use your hands to work it gently through the greens. Spread the greens out on the baking sheet and lightly season with salt. Slide both baking sheets into the oven and bake for 25–30 minutes. Keep a close eye on the carrot greens — they should be dry and crisp but not burnt.

Put the quinoa in a sieve and rinse under running water to remove any bitter compounds. Cook in a saucepan according to the package instructions until the grains swell.

Meanwhile, finely chop the hazelnuts. Briefly toast the fennel seeds in a dry pan over moderate heat. Add the hazelnuts and continue toasting until fragrant.

Zest and juice the orange for the marinade. Add both to a medium bowl with the hazelnut butter, apple cider vinegar, and mustard, stirring until smooth. Season with salt and pepper.

Add the cooked quinoa to the marinade and toss to coat. Divide between bowls and top with the carrots and carrot greens. Sprinkle with the roasted fennel seeds and hazelnuts to serve.

GREEN AND WHITE ASPARAGUS WITH CASHEW HOLLANDAISE

WHITE BEAN · WHITE WINE · NUT PARMESAN

Preheat the oven to 350°F (180°C) (convection setting). Line a baking sheet with parchment paper. Remove the woody ends of the asparagus, completely peel the white asparagus, and peel the lower third of the green asparagus if necessary. Slice the asparagus spears into roughly 2-inch (5 cm) pieces and transfer to the lined baking sheet then drizzle with some olive oil, lightly season with salt, and toss to coat. Bake for 20–25 minutes until slightly brown and tender.

Arrange the asparagus on plates and serve with cashew hollandaise and nut Parmesan.

Tastes great with:

Baby new potatoes, gnocchi, or buckwheat pasta.

***Quick and easy: Cashew hollandaise
— no cooking required***

If you are short of time, this dish can also be made with a quick version of cashew hollandaise using just a few ingredients. For this version, combine ¾ cup (150 g) of cashew butter with ⅔ cup (150 ml) of boiling water and ¼ cup (60 ml) of white wine in a medium bowl, stirring until smooth. Color the mixture with a pinch of ground turmeric and season with ½ teaspoon of kala namak (Himalayan black salt), the zest and juice of ½ a lemon, some salt, ground white pepper, and more white wine if desired.

SERVES 4

Preparation time

15 minutes + 20–25 minutes cooking time (+ 20 minutes for the cashew hollandaise + about 30 minutes for the nut Parmesan)

Kitchen equipment

Freestanding or immersion blender

For the asparagus

· 2 ¼ pounds (1 kg) asparagus (a mix of green and white)
· olive oil
· salt

Also

· cashew hollandaise (basic recipe see p. 30), to taste
· nut Parmesan (basic recipe see p. 27), to taste

THE
PECAN

Although pecans belong to the walnut family, in botanical terms they are classified as stone fruit rather than genuine nuts.

The **pecan tree**, which is a species of hickory, is a deciduous tree found predominantly in North America. It grows up to 165 feet (50 meters) and can live for more than 1,000 years. Like the walnut, it produces both male and female flowers, with pollination being done by wind.

Each **pecan nut** grows in its own green fruit husk, which acquires a dry, leathery consistency by the end of the ripening process. The smooth, thin shell is completely sealed and easy to crack. The pecan kernel is similar in shape to the walnut, and consists of two brown seed halves. It is, however, slightly slimmer than its nutty relative and has a softer consistency. These nuts were one of the staple foods for North America's indigenous people.

HEALTH BENEFITS

Pecans have a very high fat content, about 72 percent, which makes them one of the fat heavyweights among nuts, but they are rich in monounsaturated and polyunsaturated fatty acids and offer a balanced supply of minerals. They provide valuable protein (roughly 9 percent) and contain lots of essential micronutrients, including B vitamins, magnesium, zinc, calcium, potassium, and iron. Pecans have the greatest antioxidant potential of any nut.

ECONOMIC CHALLENGES

Pecans originate from the central and southern regions of North America. Today most of the global harvest still comes from the United States, primarily from Georgia, New Mexico, and Texas, as well as Mexico. Pecan trees are also now cultivated in Australia, Brazil, China, Israel, Peru, and South Africa.

As with all other nuts and agricultural produce, organic cultivation methods and a sustainable, value-added approach to farming is very important.

CULINARY USES

Pecans are used in all different ways in cooking. Thanks to their lovely shape, delicate structure, and mild, sweet flavor, they are an ideal crunchy addition to salads and vegetable dishes, or as a topping.

Fans of pecans will love using them for baking and in other sweet dishes. They taste great in cookies and cakes but are also wonderful sprinkled over muesli, rice pudding, or porridge, either just as they are or slightly caramelized.

Main cultivation areas for pecans

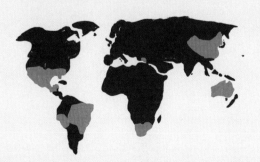

73

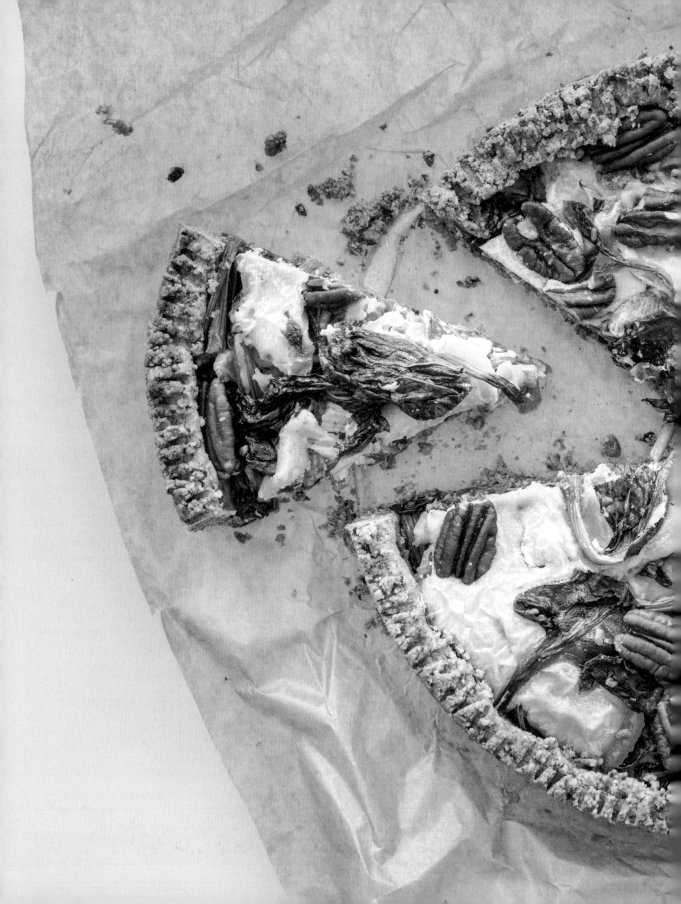

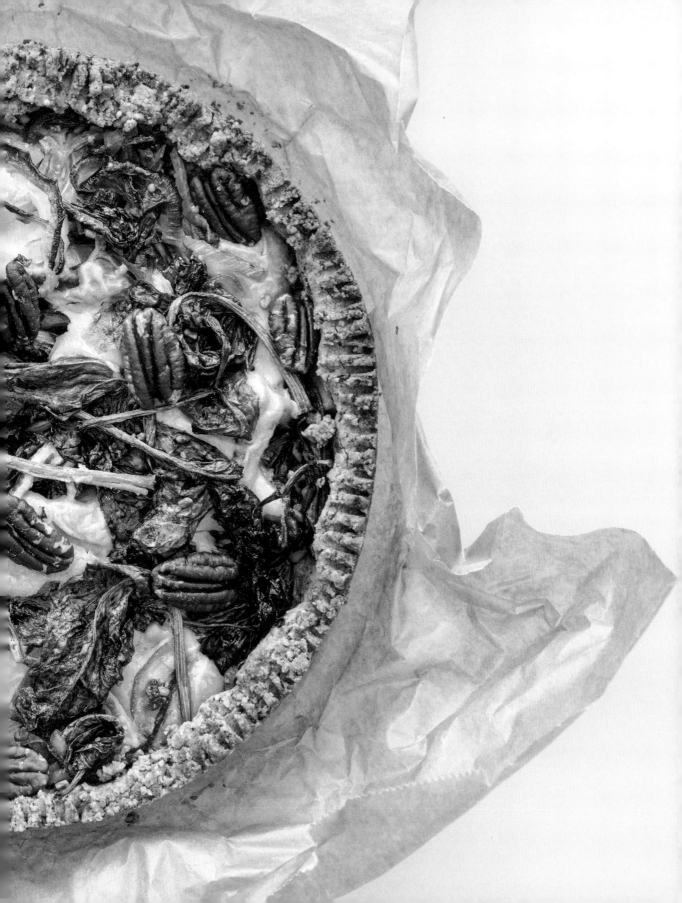

SPRING QUICHE

PUMPKIN SEED · SPINACH · FENNEL · PECAN

SERVES 4 TO 6

Preparation time
1 hour + overnight soaking +
45–55 minutes baking time

Kitchen equipment
Spice grinder, freestanding or
immersion blender, 10 to 11-inch
(25 to 28 cm) springform pan

Recipe photo see p. 74/75

Finely grind the pumpkin and sunflower seeds. Combine both with the buckwheat flour, soy flour, raw cane sugar, baking soda, and salt in a large bowl. Chop the margarine into chunks, add to the dry ingredients, and rub with your fingers to make a crumbly texture then continue working until the mixture comes together. If the pastry is too dry, add 1–2 tablespoons of cold water. Do not work the pastry for too long — the perfect consistency should be slightly crumbly and not too sticky.

Line the bottom and sides of the springform pan with parchment paper or grease with some margarine. Shape the pastry into a disc to cover the base, pressing it out to the edges and slightly up the sides to create a small rim. Chill the pastry in the fridge while the other ingredients are being prepared.

Zest and squeeze the lemon for the glaze. Drain the cashews in a sieve and rinse with cold water. Grind the nuts with the lemon zest and juice, olive oil, ⅓ cup (80 ml) of water, and a good pinch of salt, processing slowly at first and then on the highest setting, until creamy. While grinding, stir the mixture with a spoon from time to time. Gradually add up to 2 ½ tablespoons of more water. Stir in the cornstarch and season with salt and chile flakes.

Preheat the oven to 350°F (180 °C) (convection setting). For the filling, slice the fennel lengthwise in half, remove and discard the tough base, remove the green fronds, and set them aside. Slice the fennel bulb into thin strips. Peel the onion and slice very thinly into rings. Fry the fenugreek seeds in some canola oil in a large pan over moderate heat until fragrant. Add the fennel and onion and sauté briskly over high heat. Add the reserved fennel fronds and the spinach and cook until beginning to wilt. Deglaze the pan with the white wine, scraping any delicious bits from the bottom of the pan. Pour in the apple syrup and let everything caramelize slightly over moderate heat. Season with salt and pepper.

Spread the filling over the chilled base, pour over the nut glaze, and scatter the pecans on top. Bake for 45–55 minutes until the quiche is golden and the glaze has set. Let the quiche cool slightly on a wire rack before slicing.

Tastes great with:
A fresh spring salad made with different kinds of lettuce and herbs, or raw miso kohlrabi with strawberries (recipe see p. 57).

For the pastry
· 1 ¼ cups (150 g) pumpkin seeds
· ⅓ cup (50 g) sunflower seeds
· 1 cup (135 g) whole-grain buckwheat flour
· ⅓ cup (50 g) soy flour
· 2 ½ tbsp raw cane sugar
· 1 tsp baking soda
· 1 generous pinch salt
· ½ cup (140 g) cold vegan margarine + more to grease the pan

For the nut glaze
· 1 lemon
· 10 ½ ounces (300 g) cashew pieces (or whole cashews), soaked in water overnight
· 4 tbsp olive oil
· salt
· 2 ½ tbsp cornstarch
· 1–2 pinches chile flakes

For the filling
· 1 fennel bulb
· 1 red onion
· 1 tsp fenugreek seeds
· canola oil (or olive oil)
· 14 ounces (400 g) spinach
· ¼ cup (60 ml) white wine (or a light vinegar)
· 1 tbsp apple syrup (or maple syrup)
· salt
· freshly ground pepper
· 1 ¾ ounces (50 g) pecans (or walnuts or cashews)

KOHLRABI PASTA WITH CASHEW CARBONARA

MISO · TEMPEH · NUT PARMESAN

SERVES 4

Preparation time
1 hour (+ about 30 minutes for the nut Parmesan)

Kitchen equipment
Freestanding or immersion blender, spiralizer

For the cashew carbonara
· ½ cup (100 g) cashew butter
· 1 tbsp light miso (shiro miso or lupin miso)
· 1 tbsp maple syrup
· 1 tbsp nutritional yeast flakes
· ½ tsp kala namak (Himalayan black salt; available from well-stocked health food stores or online retailers)
· 1 pinch ground turmeric
· 1 pinch smoked paprika (such as Pimentón de la Vera)
· salt
· freshly ground pepper

Also
· 4 medium kohlrabi bulbs with greens
· salt
· 3 ½ ounces (100 g) tempeh
· 1 garlic clove
· 1 small red onion
· olive oil
· nut Parmesan (basic recipe see p. 27), to taste

For the cashew carbonara, blend the cashew butter, miso, maple syrup, yeast flakes, kala namak, turmeric, paprika, and ¾ cup (180 ml) of water until creamy. For a stronger "egg" flavor, add a bit more kala namak, and for a smokier flavor, add more paprika. Season with salt and pepper.

Remove the tender leaves from the kohlrabi bulbs (including the little ones in the center) and cut into very thin strips. Peel the bulbs and use a spiralizer to turn them into spaghetti. Add these to a large bowl with the kohlrabi greens, sprinkle with salt and toss to combine.

Finely dice the tempeh. Peel and finely dice the garlic and onion. Heat some olive oil in a large pan and fry the diced tempeh over moderate heat until crisp on all sides. Remove from the pan and set aside. If necessary, add some more olive oil to the pan, then sweat the onion and garlic over moderate heat until the onion is shimmering and golden. Add the carbonara sauce and stir gently until warm.

Carefully squeeze out the kohlrabi leaves and spaghetti by hand (the salt brings out the liquid and the vegetable noodles become more elastic) and add to the carbonara sauce. Scatter over the chunks of tempeh and mix well. Arrange the pasta on plates and serve with a generous sprinkling of nut Parmesan.

Tip:

This recipe can also be made with durum wheat pasta. Or why not try a combination of durum wheat and veggie spaghetti?.

ASIAN RICE NOODLE BOWL WITH ASPARAGUS

COCONUT & MISO FOAM · TOFU · FRESH HERBS

SERVES 4

Preparation time
45 minutes

Kitchen equipment
Freestanding or immersion blender

Recipe photo see p. 80/81

Finely crumble the tofu by hand into a medium bowl. Chop the herbs, including the stems, very finely and add to the bowl. Combine the rice vinegar, tamari, and ume su in a small bowl then add to the herb and tofu mixture and toss to coat. Add a dash of lime juice, if using, and season with salt and pepper.

Cook the rice noodles according to the package instructions. Meanwhile, remove the woody ends of the asparagus, peel the lower third of each spear if necessary, and cut each diagonally into thin slices. If desired, peel the ginger and deseed the chile, then slice both very thinly. Heat some coconut oil in a large pan. Briskly sauté the asparagus, ginger, and chile over high heat for 2–3 minutes then set the pan aside.

For the coconut and miso foam, blend the coconut milk, miso, cayenne, vanilla powder, salt, and ⅓ cup (80 ml) of water until very frothy.

Drain the noodles in a sieve and fold into the asparagus mixture. Divide the coconut and miso foam between four plates, arrange the asparagus and noodles on top and serve with the salsa and a sprinkling of coconut flakes.

Tip:

The miso foam has a mild yet slightly hot flavor, creating a fabulous contrast with the crisp asparagus, delicate noodles, and aromatic herb and tofu salsa. The miso foam can also be made using peanut butter or cashew butter. In this case, replace the coconut milk with ¼ cup (50 g) of nut butter and ¼ cup (60 ml) of water.

For the salsa

· 7 ounces (200 g) natural tofu
· 1 ¾ ounces (50 g) mixed fresh herbs (such as cilantro, mint, parsley, chervil, cress, or chives — I think this salsa benefits from plenty of cilantro and mint, but other herbs work well, too)
· 2 tbsp rice vinegar
· 2 tbsp tamari soy sauce (strong, dark soy sauce)
· 2 tbsp ume su (sour umeboshi seasoning; available from Asian supermarkets or health food stores)
· optional: lime juice (or lemon juice)
· salt
· freshly ground pepper

For the noodles

· 10 ounces (300 g) rice noodles
· 10 ounces (300 g) green asparagus
· 1 piece ginger, roughly 1 ½ inches (4 cm)
· 1 large fresh chile
· coconut oil (or peanut oil)

For the coconut and miso foam

· scant ½ cup (120 ml) coconut milk
· 3 tbsp light miso (shiro miso or lupin miso)
· 1 pinch cayenne pepper
· 1 pinch bourbon vanilla powder
· 1 pinch salt

Also

· 4 tbsp toasted unsweetened coconut flakes

SWEET CARROT HALVA

CARDAMOM · VANILLA · SESAME BRITTLE

SERVES 4

Preparation time

25 minutes + 20 minutes cooking
time + 10 minutes cooling time

Kitchen equipment

Freestanding or immersion
blender

Ingredients

· 14 ounces (400 g) carrots
· 1 pinch salt
· 4 tbsp maple syrup
· 3 tbsp light tahini + more to serve
· ½ tsp ground cardamom
· 1 pinch bourbon vanilla powder
· ¼ cup (50 g) white cane sugar
· ⅓ cup (50 g) sesame seeds

Bring a small amount of water to a gentle boil in a medium saucepan. Finely slice the carrots and cook in the gently simmering water for 20 minutes until very soft.

Drain the carrots in a sieve and purée with the salt until creamy. Mix in the maple syrup and tahini and flavor with the cardamom and vanilla powder. Divide the halva between bowls and set aside.

To prepare for making the sesame brittle, line a large plate with parchment paper. Cook the white cane sugar in a small nonstick pan over moderate to high heat. As soon as the sugar begins to melt (at first it will melt slowly, but this soon speeds up), let it caramelize, while stirring constantly with a wooden spoon. Remember, both the pan and the liquid caramel are too hot to use a rubber spatula or to allow tasting. Quickly stir in the sesame seeds and as soon as they begin to color, pour the mixture onto the lined plate and spread out thinly. After about 10 minutes, the brittle will be firm and can be broken into pieces.

Crumble the sesame brittle over the halva and serve each portion with a blob of tahini.

Tip:

Halva also tastes great chilled and can easily be prepared a few hours or even days in advance. It will keep covered in the refrigerator for about 4 days.

CASHEW AND COCONUT MOUSSE

ELDERFLOWER · LEMON

Melt the cocoa butter in a small saucepan. Zest and juice the lemon.

Drain the cashews and coconut flakes in a sieve and rinse with cold water. Blend both with the lemon zest and juice, elderflower syrup, and ⅓ cup (80 ml) of water, processing everything on the highest setting until the purée thickens. If necessary, add a bit more water and process again. It will take a few minutes to create a thick and creamy mixture. Keep processing on low and add the melted cocoa butter.

Transfer the cashew and coconut mousse to a medium bowl. You can add agave syrup if the mixture isn't sweet enough. Stir in the coconut flour and salt using a balloon whisk. Cover the mousse and let set overnight in the refrigerator.

To serve, use two dessert spoons to scoop out portions of the mousse. Put two to three scoops on a dessert plate, drizzle with elderflower syrup and scatter with edible petals.

SERVES 4 TO 6

Preparation time
30 minutes + overnight soaking and cooling time

Kitchen equipment
Freestanding or immersion blender

Ingredients
· 1 ¾ ounces (50 g) cocoa butter
· 1 lemon
· 3 ½ ounces (100 g) cashew pieces (or whole cashews), soaked in water overnight
· 3 ½ ounces (100 g) unsweetened coconut flakes, soaked in water overnight
· 3–4 tbsp elderflower syrup + some extra to drizzle
· optional: 2 tbsp agave syrup
· ¾ cup (100 g) coconut flour
· 1 pinch salt
· dried edible flowers to decorate

SUMMER

What makes summer special? The bright morning light streaming in through the treetops at the crack of dawn, the warm evening breeze tempting us to lay a table to dine outdoors. Only once the heat of the day has diminished does our appetite return. An abundance of delicious seasonal vegetables and fresh herbs are on offer. The distinctive aroma of barbecued food wafts over, as we enjoy a glass of full-bodied red wine and make the most of the long summer days.

NICE CREAM BERRY BOWL

BANANA · BLUEBERRY · DATE · MACADAMIA

Freeze the bananas and berries for the nice cream overnight: First peel the bananas and break into chunks the size of ice cubes. Freeze these chunks and the berries in a freezer safe dish. Soak the dates in water in a small bowl overnight.

Remove the bananas and berries from the freezer and let defrost briefly. Meanwhile, roughly chop the macadamias for the topping.

Purée the slightly thawed bananas and berries with the dates and their soaking water until the consistency of spreadable ice cream. Break up the frozen mixture with a spoon every so often during this process.

Divide the nice cream between small bowls or glasses and smooth out slightly. Sprinkle with macadamia nuts and blueberries for serving.

SERVES 4

Preparation time
15 minutes + overnight chilling and soaking

Kitchen equipment
Freestanding mixer

For the nice cream
· 4 very ripe bananas
· about 14 ounces (400 g) blueberries (or raspberries)
· 4 dates, pitted

For the topping
· about 4 tbsp macadamia nuts
· about 4 tbsp blueberries (or 2 tbsp dried cranberries)

Did you know:

Nice cream bowls make a fantastic summer breakfast or a refreshing snack after a bike ride or hike. You can also use other kinds of frozen fruit and sprinkle the dish with whatever appeals. Absolutely delicious!

DULCE DE CAFÉ

COFFEE · CASHEW · COCONUT · SALT

MAKES 1 LARGE JAR

Preparation time
10 minutes

Kitchen equipment
Freestanding or immersion
blender

Ingredients
· 3 tbsp coconut oil
· 2 ounces (60 g) coconut butter
  (creamed coconut)
· ⅓ cup (80 ml) rice milk
· 4 ¼ ounces (120 g) cashew butter
  (or another pale nut butter)
· 4 ¼ tbsp rice syrup
· ½ tsp ground espresso
· 1 generous pinch salt
· 1 pinch bourbon vanilla powder

Melt the coconut oil and coconut butter by placing them in a bowl suspended over a pan of simmering water.

Purée the liquid coconut mixture with the rice milk, cashew butter, rice syrup, espresso, salt, and vanilla powder until smooth and creamy. Add more salt and vanilla powder, as needed, then transfer to a clean, airtight glass jar.

Tip:

Dulce de café is ideal as a topping for muffins (recipe see p. 95), chocolate ice cream, or blancmange. It also tastes fantastic spread on bread. Store the cream in the refrigerator (it will become slightly firmer) and use within 8 days as it contains no preservatives.

TIGER NUT AND OAT MUFFINS WITH A COFFEE AND CASHEW TOPPING

ALMOND · CHERRY · VANILLA

In a large bowl, combine the tiger nut flour, oat flour, cornstarch, raw cane sugar, baking powder, baking soda, salt, and vanilla powder.

Zest and juice the lemon. Add the lemon zest and juice, ⅓ cup (80 ml) of the oat milk, the almond butter, and apple-sauce to the dry ingredients and whisk until smooth. If the mixture is too thick, add the remaining oat milk. Fold in the cherries.

Preheat the oven to 325°F (160°C) (convection setting). Line a muffin pan with paper liners. Spoon the batter into the muffin cups and bake for 25–30 minutes until lightly brown. Let the muffins cool briefly in the pan, then transfer to a wire rack and let cool completely.

Cover the cooled muffins with some dulce de café and decorate with coffee beans, if using, to serve.

MAKES 12 MUFFINS

Preparation time
35 minutes + 25–30 minutes baking + cooling time

Kitchen equipment
Hand mixer or stand mixer, muffin pan

For the muffins
· 1 ¼ cups (150 g) tiger nut flour
· 1 ¾ (150 g) (gluten-free) oat flour
· ⅓ cup (40 g) cornstarch
· 5 tbsp raw cane sugar
· 1 tbsp baking powder
· ½ tsp baking soda
· 1 pinch salt
· 1 pinch bourbon vanilla powder
· 1 lemon
· ⅓–⅔ cup (80–150 ml) oat milk
· ⅓ cup (80 g) almond butter
· 2 tbsp applesauce
· 5 ounces (150 g fresh or frozen) cherries, pitted

For the topping
· dulce de café (recipe see p. 92)
· optional: coffee beans

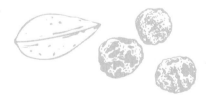

THE
BRAZIL NUT

Brazil nuts are the seeds from a capsule fruit.

The **Brazil nut tree** belongs to the Lecythidace-ae family and is one of the largest primeval trees in South America. It reaches a height of almost 200 feet (60 meters) and grows wild mainly in the Brazilian and Bolivian rainforest, in Peru, and in Ivory Coast.

Brazil nuts ripen in groups of about 20 seeds in a **pod** that's much like a coconut. Each nut is also enclosed in its own hard shell. The kernel itself is slightly elongated and triangular. When mature, the fruit pods fall to the ground and are collected.

HEALTH BENEFITS

Brazil nuts are among the nuts with the highest fat content, about 70 percent, but in exchange, they are absolutely packed with minerals. In addition to lots of unsaturated fatty acids, which protect our blood vessels and the cardiovascular system, Brazil nuts supply all sorts of vital micronutrients and vitamins, including phosphorus, potassium, magnesium, calcium, iron, zinc, and vitamin E.

These nuts are particularly coveted for their high selenium content. This is a trace element that supports thyroid function and boosts the immune system, and it is not found in this form in any other food. However, to produce nuts that are high in selenium, Brazil nut trees need to grow in selenium-rich soil. When this is the case, just 1 to 3 Brazil nuts each day will satisfy your daily selenium requirements.

ECONOMIC CHALLENGES

Brazil nut trees grow best in the tropical regions of South America. Only orchid bees are strong enough to forge their way through the heavy petals of the blossom to spread the pollen contained within. The nuts are spread by a type of rodent that looks rather like a squirrel and is native to the rainforest. Due to their dependence on these specific animal species, it is difficult to cultivate Brazil nut trees elsewhere.

The trees also grow very slowly: It can sometimes take 12 years for the first flowers to appear, and as many as 20 to 30 years for the first nuts to be produced. The harvesting period is in the middle of the rainy season, which makes it difficult for collectors to access the trees. The collected nuts are quickly prepared for drying to stop them from developing mold. In other words, before Brazil nuts can be sold, there are various obstacles to overcome. Guaranteed, reasonable purchase prices for Brazil nuts are absolutely essential, as protecting the trees is hugely important for the people who depend on harvesting the nuts. If the trees can offer a reliable income and a viable future, the local population will be more invested in preserving the rainforest. In this sense, Brazil nuts can help save the rainforest.

CULINARY USES

Brazil nuts are particularly useful in savory recipes. Thanks to their crunch, they retain their bite in nut roasts and Bolognese sauces, ensuring a unique chewy texture. They have an intensely nutty and slightly buttery flavor, without being bitter (as walnuts can sometimes be) nor particularly sweet (like hazelnuts or almonds). And when combined with other nuts, they add a delightful crunch that works well in sweet treats, too.

Main cultivation areas for Brazil nuts

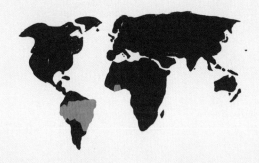

CARIBBEAN SWEET POTATO SOUP

MANGO · CHILE · PEANUT · BANANA CHIP

SERVES 4

Preparation time

45 minutes + 25 minutes
cooking time

Kitchen equipment

Freestanding or immersion
blender

For the soup

· 1 piece ginger, roughly 1 ½ inches
(4 cm)
· 1 piece turmeric, roughly 1 ½
inches (4 cm)
· 7 ounces (200 g) parsnip
· 1 ¼ pounds (600 g) sweet potato
· 7 ounces (200 g) mango (or 3
ounces (90 g) dried mango, soaked
in boiling water for 15 minutes)
· 2 tbsp coconut oil
· 1 tsp ground cumin
· 1 tsp curry powder
· salt
· 2–4 tbsp rice vinegar (or another
pale vinegar)
· freshly ground pepper

For the topping

· 1–2 passion fruit (or a couple
cubes of mango)
· 1 handful fresh cilantro leaves
· 1 fresh chile
· 3 ½ ounces (100 g) banana chips
· 3 ½ ounces (100 g) salted roasted
peanuts

Finely chop the ginger and turmeric for the soup. Peel and dice the parsnip and sweet potato. Peel and dice the flesh of the mango.

Heat the coconut oil in a large saucepan. Sauté the chopped ginger and turmeric briefly over moderate heat, then add the parsnip and sweet potato and sprinkle with cumin and curry powder. Continue frying for about 3 minutes then add the mango and 3 ⅓ cups (800 ml) of water. Add a bit of salt and bring to a boil. Cover the pan, reduce the heat to low, and simmer for about 25 minutes until tender.

Meanwhile, for the topping, slice the passion fruit in half and scoop out the contents. Roughly chop the cilantro, slice the chile diagonally into thin rings, removing the seeds if preferred.

Purée the soup until smooth then season with rice vinegar, salt, and pepper. Divide between deep bowls and garnish with the chile, banana chips, peanuts, cilantro, and passion fruit.

BEAN AND ORANGE HUMMUS

SESAME SEED · CHILE · GARLIC

For the hummus, peel and roughly chop the garlic. Put the beans in a sieve and rinse with cold water. Purée the beans, rice vinegar, and orange zest and juice until thick and creamy. Add the olive oil, tahini, garlic, and chile flakes and season with maple syrup, salt, and pepper.

Spoon the bean and orange hummus into a medium bowl and smooth the surface with the back of the spoon. Garnished with sesame seeds, chile flakes, and nigella seeds and serve with rice crackers

Tastes great with:

A glass of chilled white wine or rice wine as an aperitif.

SERVES 4

Preparation time
15 minutes

Kitchen equipment
Freestanding or immersion blender

For the hummus
· 1 garlic clove
· 8 ½ ounces (240 g) canned or jarred white beans (drained weight)
· 5 tbsp rice vinegar
· zest of 1 orange
· ⅓ cup (80 ml) orange juice
· 5 tbsp olive oil (or sesame oil)
· 5 tbsp tahini
· ½ tsp chile flakes (or cayenne pepper)
· 1 tbsp maple syrup (or coconut sugar)
· salt
· freshly ground pepper

For the topping
· sesame seeds
· chile flakes
· nigella seeds
· Asian rice crackers

CASHEW MOZZARELLA WITH MANGO AND FENNEL SALAD

ARUGULA · CHILE · PUMPKIN SEED

SERVES 4

Preparation time

30 minutes (+ 15–45 minutes for the mozzarella, depending on the variety + overnight soaking + 8–24 hours fermentation + possibly 8 hours cooling time)

For the salad

· 1 ripe but not too soft mango
· ½ fennel bulb
· 1 fresh chile
· 3 ½ ounces (100 g) pumpkin seeds
· 1 bunch arugula
· 1 tbsp coarsely ground red Kampot pepper
· 4–8 balls cashew mozzarella (basic recipe for mozzarella with psyllium husks or tapioca flour see p. 26/27)

For the dressing

· optional: 1 garlic clove
· 5 tbsp fruity extra-virgin olive oil
· 5 tbsp balsamic vinegar
· 3–4 tbsp maple syrup
· salt

For the salad, peel the mango and cut the flesh of the fruit into strips using a peeler. Remove the tough base of the fennel. Cut the bulb into very thin slices then dice. Thinly slice the chile into rings, removing the seeds if preferred.

Toast the pumpkin seeds in a small dry pan over moderate heat until they begin to pop.

For the dressing, peel the garlic and chop very finely, if using. In a small bowl, combine the olive oil, balsamic vinegar, maple syrup, 5 tbsp of water, and the garlic, if using. Season with salt.

Remove the stems from the arugula and put the leaves in a large bowl with the mango, fennel, chile, and Kampot pepper. Drizzle with the dressing, mix, and leave to infuse briefly. Carefully tear or chop the mozzarella into pieces and fold gently into the salad. Divide the salad between plates and serve scattered with roasted pumpkin seeds.

Tastes great with:

Freshly toasted bread. This salad is also delicious served with rice noodles.

CAULIFLOWER TABBOULEH

CUCUMBER · CASHEW · THYME

SERVES 4 TO 6

Preparation time
50 minutes + 30–45 minutes
cooking time

Kitchen equipment
Food processor and freestanding
or immersion blender

Recipe photo see p. 106/107

Preheat the oven to 325°F (160°C) (convection setting). Remove the leaves and the lower part of the stalk from the cauliflower, setting aside any presentable leaves to make chips. Split the cauliflower into florets and roughly chop the top part of the stalk. Chop the florets and stalk in the food processor until the cauliflower looks like couscous.

Dice the cucumber very finely. Chop the parsley very finely, including the stems, and strip the thyme leaves off the stems. Zest and juice the lemon. Combine the cauliflower couscous, cucumber, parsley, thyme, lemon zest and juice in a large bowl. Leave to infuse while preparing the other ingredients.

To make the marinade for the chips, stir together the olive oil, tamari, maple syrup, and salt in a small bowl. Grease a baking sheet with olive oil, spread out the cauliflower leaves and lightly brush with the marinade. Bake for 30–45 minutes, turning the leaves every 10 minutes, until crispy. Pour the remaining marinade over the cauliflower tabbouleh and mix.

Meanwhile, for the cashew sour cream, roughly chop the silken tofu, crumble the natural tofu, and purée both with the cashews until well combined. Add the canola oil, apple cider vinegar, and mustard and process for 3 minutes on a moderate to high setting so the mixture emulsifies to create a light sour cream. Season with salt, pepper, and kala namak, if using, for a slightly "eggy" flavor.

Arrange the cauliflower tabbouleh on plates with the chips and add generous dollops of cashew sour cream.

Tastes great with:
Warm polenta or potatoes.

For the tabbouleh
· 1 large cauliflower
· 1 cucumber
· 2 bunches fresh parsley
· 2–4 sprigs fresh thyme
· 1 lemon

For the marinade
· 5 tbsp olive oil + more to grease
  the baking sheet
· 5 tbsp tamari soy sauce (strong,
  dark soy sauce)
· 3–4 tbsp maple syrup
· 1 tsp salt

For the cashew sour cream
· 7 ounces (200 g) silken tofu
· 3 ½ ounces (100 g) natural tofu
· 3 ½ ounces (100 g) cashew pieces
  (or whole cashews)
· 5 tbsp mild canola oil
· 2 tbsp apple cider vinegar
· 1 tsp mustard
· salt
· freshly ground pepper
· optional: 1 pinch kala namak
  (Himalayan black salt, available
  from well-stocked health food
  stores or online retailers)

THE
CASHEW

Strictly speaking, cashews are not nuts but a type of stone fruit.

The **cashew tree** belongs to the sumac family and is a fast-growing, leafy evergreen that loves tropical climates and is adept at surviving periods of drought.

Each **cashew kernel** grows individually on a thick pedicel, which is known as the **cashew apple** and resembles an inverted bell pepper in shape. Once the cashew kernel is ripe, the cashew apple turns a golden orange or red color and develops an intensely fruity fragrance. Cashew apples have a sweet but tart flavor and are rich in vitamin C. Unfortunately, they are so del-

icate when ripe that they cannot be exported after the cashew kernel has been harvested. In countries where cashews are grown, the cashew apple is processed to make juice, jam, liquor, or Cajuína, a drink that is said to have health properties.

The **cashew** itself is a hard, kidney-shaped "nut" that surrounds the kernel that we are familiar with. It contains an oil that is an irritant to skin and must be destroyed through heat during roasting. This makes the process of peeling cashews laborious and time-consuming.

HEALTH BENEFITS

Cashews are rich in monounsaturated and poly-unsaturated fatty acids, which have a positive impact on the cardiovascular system and cholesterol levels. The nuts consist of roughly 45 percent fat, 20 percent protein, and 30 percent carbohydrates.

Cashews contain lots of valuable vitamins and minerals, such as B vitamins, vitamin K, vitamin E, magnesium, and phosphorus. Another characteristic worth highlighting is a uniquely high level of tryptophan, which the body converts into the "happiness" hormone serotonin, thus contributing to our well-being.

ECONOMIC CHALLENGES

Cashews travel a long way before arriving on our supermarket shelves. They are mainly cultivated in Ivory Coast, in Burundi, Tanzania, Mali, Kenya, Mozambique, and Nigeria, as well as in India, Vietnam, Brazil, and the Philippines. Unfortunately, cashews suffer from the same problem as coffee and chocolate: All too often the value-added chain is not completed in the countries where they are grown. The unshelled nuts are bought cheaply from farmers after harvesting then shipped to Indonesia, Vietnam, or India to be shelled using machinery or manually by poorly paid workers in degrading conditions. The reality of this work has been documented in images of hands burned by the toxic oil contained in the shells.

Cashews that have been cultivated in accordance with organic and fair trade standards might be slightly more expensive, but they're worth it. They guarantee added value in the country of origin, ensure better conditions for producers, protect the environment, and support the development and expansion of local infrastructure.

CULINARY USES

Due to their slightly sweet but relatively neutral flavor compared with other nuts, cashews are particularly good for making nut milk products, raw vegan cakes, delicious mousses, and other desserts. The nuts can be baked or toasted whole, ground to make nut Parmesan, and scattered over salads. Cashew butter can be used to thicken sweet or savory sauces and creamy dips.

Main cultivation areas for cashews

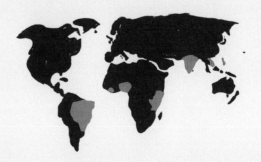

OVEN-ROASTED BELL PEPPER AND APRICOT SALAD

SAGE · CAPER · SESAME SEED · PINE NUT

SERVES 4

Preparation time
40 minutes

For the oven-roasted salad
· 4 yellow bell peppers
· 4 sprigs fresh sage
· olive oil
· 4 apricots
· 1 lemon
· 2 tbsp capers

For the dressing
· 5 tbsp high-quality mature
  balsamic vinegar
· 5 tbsp olive oil
· 2 tbsp light tahini (or blanched
  almond butter)
· 1 tbsp apricot jam (or maple syrup)
· 1 pinch cayenne pepper
· ½ tsp salt

Also
· 3 ½ ounces (100 g) pine nuts
· freshly ground pepper

Preheat the oven to 350 °F (180 °C) (convection setting). Line a baking sheet with parchment paper. Slice the bell peppers in half, remove the stalk and seeds, and cut into wide strips. Remove the sage leaves from the stalk and transfer to the lined baking sheet, along with the strips of bell pepper. Drizzle everything with olive oil and bake for 15 minutes.

Meanwhile, halve the apricots, remove the stone, and slice into quarters. Slice the lemon crosswise into thin rounds and then slice into strips. When the peppers have baked for 15 minutes, add the apricots, lemon strips, and capers, toss to combine, and continue baking for another 15 minutes, then allow to cool slightly.

Stir together the balsamic vinegar, olive oil, tahini, apricot jam, cayenne pepper, and salt in a small bowl. Add some water as needed to make sure the consistency is creamy and not too thick. Gently toast the pine nuts in a small dry pan over moderate heat.

Arrange the warm, oven-roasted ingredients on a large platter. Drizzle with the dressing, season generously with pepper, and serve scattered with pine nuts.

Tastes great with:

Toasted bread (as a starter), or pasta or couscous (as a main course).

WILD TOMATOES WITH EGGPLANT BACON

BRAZIL NUT · GARLIC · SMOKED SALT

Chop or slice the tomatoes. If using, peel the onion and slice very thinly into rings. Arrange both on a large platter and sprinkle with salt and balsamic vinegar.

Remove the stem of the eggplant and dice the flesh very finely. Heat a generous quantity of olive oil in a medium skillet. Briskly sauté the diced eggplant over high heat for 5–8 minutes, stirring constantly, until nicely browned on all sides. Season with the smoked paprika and smoked salt. Scatter the eggplant bacon over the tomatoes. Sprinkle with Kampot pepper and drizzle everything once more with balsamic vinegar. Garnish with basil leaves, if using.

Chop the Brazil nuts, peel and finely slice the garlic. Heat some olive oil in a small pan and sauté the garlic and nuts over moderate heat. Season with the sweet paprika and salt, then deglaze the pan with the tamari, scraping any delicious bits from the bottom of the pan. Add the maple syrup and caramelize slightly. Serve the salad scattered with the crunchy brazil nut and garlic topping.

SERVES 4

Preparation time
45 minutes

Kitchen equipment
Freestanding or immersion blender

Ingredients
· 1 ¾ pounds (800 g) colorful wild tomatoes
· optional: 1 red onion
· salt
· high-quality mature balsamic vinegar
· 1 large eggplant
· olive oil
· 1 tsp smoked paprika (such as Pimentón de la Vera)
· smoked salt
· coarsely ground black Kampot pepper (or freshly ground black pepper)
· optional: 5–8 sprigs fresh basil
· 3 ½ ounces (100 g) Brazil nuts
· 2 garlic cloves
· ½ tsp sweet paprika
· 2 tbsp tamari soy sauce (strong dark soy sauce)
· 2 tbsp maple syrup

Tastes great with:
Pizza bread or crisp toasted baguette.

WARM SUGAR SNAP PEA AND APPLE SALAD

SHALLOT · WALNUT · ANISEED

SERVES 4

Preparation time
50 minutes

Ingredients
· 14 ounces (400 g) sugar snap peas
· salt
· 3 shallots
· 2 tart apples
· canola oil (or another oil suitable for frying)
· 1 tsp coriander seeds
· 1 tsp aniseeds
· 3 ½ ounces (100 g) walnuts
· 1 ¾ ounces (50 g) apple chips
· 5 tbsp walnut oil
· 5 tbsp tamari soy sauce (strong dark soy sauce)
· 5 tbsp apple cider vinegar
· 3–4 tbsp apple syrup (or maple syrup)
· 1 tbsp Bavarian sweet mustard
· chile flakes
· freshly ground pepper
· 2–4 tbsp high-quality mature wine vinegar

Clean the sugar snap peas. If there are any more mature pods, open them and remove the peas. Bring plenty of water to a boil in a large saucepan and salt generously. Fill a large bowl with ice water. Blanch the sugar snap pods and any loose peas for 3–5 minutes. Drain the pods and peas and immerse briefly in the ice water so they retain their vibrant green color. Drain the cooled pods and peas in a sieve and set aside in a large bowl.

Peel the shallots and cut each into eight slices. Quarter and core the apples then cut into slices. In a large pan (or wok), heat plenty of canola oil and briefly sauté the coriander and aniseed over moderate heat. Add the shallots and fry briskly until starting to brown. Add the sliced apple, season generously with salt, cover the pan, and continue cooking over moderate heat for 5–8 minutes.

Meanwhile, roughly chop the walnuts and toast in a small dry pan until fragrant and lightly browned. Chop the apple chips into slightly smaller pieces.

Whisk together the walnut oil, tamari, apple cider vinegar, apple syrup, and mustard in a small bowl to make a dressing. Add the apple and shallot mixture to the sugar snap peas and pour over the dressing. Gently mix everything together, seasoning with chile flakes and pepper.

Divide the sugar snap and apple mixture between plates and scatter with walnuts and apple chips then drizzle with wine vinegar to serve.

STUFFED ZUCCHINI FLOWERS WITH MACADAMIA AND CASHEW RICOTTA

PEACH · MINT

For the nut ricotta, drain the nuts in a sieve and rinse with cold water. Purée the nuts with about ⅓ cup (80 ml) of water until thick and creamy. Add the lemon juice, miso, probiotic powder, mustard, and nutmeg then mix and season with salt.

Transfer the mixture to a nut milk bag and place this in a sieve suspended over a bowl. Leave to mature and drain at room temperature for 8–12 hours. Tip the fermented nut ricotta into a medium bowl and season with salt, olive oil, and white wine vinegar.

Halve the peaches, remove the stones, and cut into slices. Pick the mint leaves off the stems. Very carefully, open the zucchini flowers, put 1 generous teaspoon of the macadamia and cashew ricotta into each one and gently close it again. Heat plenty of olive oil in a large pan and briefly sauté the sliced peaches over high heat. Reduce the heat and carefully lie the zucchini flowers on top of the peaches. Continue cooking for 1–2 minutes until the zucchini flowers start to brown slightly on the bottom but are not falling apart.

Divide the zucchini flowers and peaches between plates and season with salt and pepper. Serve scattered with mint and drizzled with olive oil and white wine vinegar.

Tastes great with:
Crisply toasted slices of baguette.

Tip:
If zucchini flowers are only available along with whole zucchini, the vegetables can also be stuffed and served alongside or turned into zucchini pasta the following day (recipe see p. 126).

SERVES 4

Preparation time
50 minutes + overnight soaking + 8–12 hours fermentation time

Kitchen equipment
Freestanding or immersion blender, nut milk bag

For the nut ricotta
· 3 ½ ounces (100 g) cashew pieces (or whole cashews), soaked in water overnight
· 3 ½ ounces (100 g) macadamia nuts, soaked in water overnight
· 2 tbsp lemon juice
· 2 tbsp shiro miso
· ½ tsp probiotic powder (such as OMNi-BiOTiC®, VSL#3®, or a different probiotic powder or capsule, available at drugstores)
· ½ tsp mustard
· 1 pinch ground nutmeg
· salt
· 1–2 tbsp olive oil
· 1–2 tbsp mild white wine vinegar

Also
· 4 large peaches
· 1 bunch fresh mint
· 12–16 zucchini flowers
· olive oil
· salt
· freshly ground pepper
· mild white wine vinegar

MILLET RISOTTO WITH ARTICHOKES

HAZELNUT MAYONNAISE · LEMON · BLACK MUSTARD SEED

SERVES 4

Preparation time
1 hour 10 minutes

Kitchen equipment
Freestanding or immersion blender

Recipe photo see p. 122/123

To make the mayonnaise, blend the dates, yogurt, hazelnut butter, apple cider vinegar, mustard, salt, and paprika until smooth. Season with additional salt and paprika, if desired — it should be spicy and aromatic. With the blender running, add the vegetable oil in a thin stream, blending until the mixture starts to thicken. Divide the mayonnaise between four small dishes and keep in the refrigerator.

To cook the artichokes, bring plenty of water to a boil in a large, wide saucepan. Slice the lemon crosswise into rounds and add to the water, along with the bay leaves and salt. Remove the artichoke stalks, either using a sharp knife to cut the stalk immediately below the base of the flower or simply snap them off. Remove the dry outer leaves and trim any brown tips with a sharp pair of scissors. Place the artichoke heads next to each other in the boiling water, cover the pan, and cook over moderate heat for 30–40 minutes until the leaves pull away easily.

Meanwhile, put the millet in a sieve, rinse with hot water and leave to drain. Peel and very finely dice the onion and garlic. Heat the olive oil in a large saucepan and sauté the mustard seeds over moderate heat until they begin to pop. Add the diced onion and garlic and sauté briskly over high heat, then add the millet and continue frying, stirring constantly, until it begins to stick to the bottom of the pan.

Deglaze the pan with the white wine, scraping any delicious bits from the bottom of pan, and lightly season with salt. Pour in a third of the vegetable broth and bring to a boil, then reduce the heat and simmer gently, stirring occasionally and adding a bit more vegetable broth as it's absorbed by the millet. Continue simmering until the millet is tender.

Remove the artichokes from the water and let drain in a sieve. Roughly chop the hazelnuts and quarter the lemon. Divide the millet risotto between plates, lightly season with pepper, and scatter with the hazelnuts. Place the artichokes alongside, drizzle with lemon juice, and serve each plate with a little dish of the mayonnaise.

For the hazelnut mayonnaise
· 2 Medjool dates, pitted
· ¾ cup (200 g) soy yogurt
· ¼ cup (50 g) hazelnut butter
· 2 tbsp apple cider vinegar (or a mild white wine vinegar or lemon juice)
· 1 tsp spicy mustard
· 1 tsp salt
· 1 pinch smoked paprika (such as Pimentón de la Vera)
· ⅓ cup (80 ml) neutral vegetable oil

For the artichokes
· 1 lemon
· 2–4 bay leaves
· 1 tsp salt
· 4 large artichokes

For the millet risotto
· 1 ½ cups (300 g) golden millet
· 1 small onion
· 1 garlic clove
· 2–4 tbsp olive oil
· 1 tsp black mustard seeds
· ⅓ cup (80 ml) white wine
· salt
· 2 ½ to 3 ⅓ cups (600 to 800 ml) vegetable broth (or water)

Also
· 1 ¾ ounces (50 g) roasted hazelnuts
· 1 lemon
· freshly ground pepper

RAW ZUCCHINI PASTA BOLOGNESE

FENNEL · CARROT · PECAN · SUNFLOWER SEED

SERVES 4

Preparation time
40 minutes (+ about 30 minutes
for the nut Parmesan)

Kitchen equipment
Spiralizer, freestanding or
immersion blender

Ingredients
· 2–4 firm zucchini (14–20 ounces /
  400–600 g)
· salt
· optional: some lemon juice
· 3 ½ ounces (100 g) sunflower
  seeds
· 3 ½ ounces (100 g) canned or
  jarred chickpeas (drained weight)
· ½ fennel bulb (or 3 celery sticks)
· 1 carrot
· 4 juicy tomatoes (roughly
  14 ounces / 400 g)
· 1 sprig each fresh oregano,
  marjoram, rosemary, and thyme
· 5 tbsp olive oil
· ¼ cup (60 g) tomato paste
· 2 tbsp tamari soy sauce (strong,
  dark soy sauce)
· 2 tbsp maple syrup
· 1 ¾ ounces (50 g) pecans
· freshly ground pepper
· nut Parmesan (basic recipe see
  p. 27), to taste
· 1 handful fresh basil leaves

Use a spiralizer to turn the zucchini into spaghetti. Transfer to a large bowl, season lightly with salt, and drizzle with lemon juice, if using. Gently toss then set aside.

Toast the sunflower seeds in a small dry pan over moderate heat. Put the chickpeas in a sieve and rinse with cold water. Remove the tough base of the fennel bulb, then very finely dice or grate the fennel and carrot. Roughly chop the tomatoes. Strip the herbs from the stems.

Purée the tomatoes, olive oil, tomato paste, tamari, and maple syrup to make a sauce. Add the sunflower seeds, chickpeas, fennel, carrot, herbs, and pecans, then pulse until you have a chunky bolognese sauce. Season with salt and pepper.

Meanwhile, water will have been drawn from the zucchini pasta, which will be much more flexible. Drain the zucchini pasta in a sieve and combine in batches with some of the bolognese sauce in a large bowl. Divide between plates and serve each portion with a bit more sauce, nut Parmesan and basil leaves.

Tip:

Retain and refrigerate the water from the chickpeas (aquafaba) because it makes an excellent substitute for whipped egg whites. Whisk the aquafaba until stiff, just as you would with egg whites, then combine with melted dark chocolate to make mousse au chocolat, or with a light nut butter to make coconut and cardamom mousse (recipe see p. 134).

THE
TIGER NUT

In botanical terms, the tiger nut — also known as the earth almond or chufa — is not a nut; it is the tuber from a grass-like plant.

The **tiger nut plant** belongs to the sedge family, also known as the Cyperaceae family. This herbaceous plant grows to about 24 inches (60 centimeters) in height and is found between the tropics and subtropics and as far as North America.

The **tiger nut** itself grows as a tuberous bulge on the root system underground. The round brown tubers are the size of a pea and very oily. They are cleaned after harvesting and dried for about three months before being sold as whole nuts or ground to make tiger nut flour.

HEALTH BENEFITS

Tiger nuts have a fat content of about 25 percent, which is much lower than other nuts. Even peanuts (which are really legumes) consist of almost 50 percent fat.

As well as supplying lots of unsaturated fatty acids, tiger nuts contain valuable carbohydrates and plenty of dietary fiber. Their high fiber content gives tiger nuts prebiotic qualities, with a beneficial effect on digestion. They are also packed with all sorts of micronutrients, including vitamins C and E, potassium, iron, magnesium, and zinc.

ECONOMIC CHALLENGES

Tiger nuts are thought to originate from the Mediterranean region and western Asia. Today they are mainly grown in southern Europe, particularly in the Spanish region of Valencia, and in northern and western Africa. They require sandy, noncalcareous clay soil and a mild climate. Other than this, tiger nuts are relatively undemanding, which is why they've gradually found their way into all sorts of countries and latitudes and have the potential to threaten native plants. In fact, some botanists regard them as the very worst weed due to the way they have taken root so successfully and are threatening local species in countries such as Switzerland and the Netherlands.

CULINARY USES

The regional specialty horchata de chufa is a sweet tiger nut milk that is particularly popular in Spain. Tiger nuts are usually sold as flakes or flour. Thanks to their slightly sweet, vanilla flavor — similar to almonds — tiger nuts are ideal for baking and taste great in sweet treats, such as cakes and banana bread. Their mild nutty flavor also adds a bit of interest to muesli.

Main cultivation areas for tiger nuts

MINI CHOCOLATE CAKES WITH OLIVE OIL

TIGER NUT · GRAPEFRUIT

Combine the tiger nut flour, cornstarch, baking powder, and salt in a medium bowl. Grease the cake pans with olive oil. Preheat the oven to 350°F (180°C) (convection setting).

Break or chop the chocolate into little pieces and melt in a bowl suspended over a pan of simmering water. Whisk the olive oil and plant-based milk into the melted chocolate. Add the dry ingredients and mix until smooth. Divide the mixture evenly between the cake pans and bake for about 20 minutes.

Meanwhile, segment the grapefruit. To do this, peel the grapefruit, removing all the white pith. Cut between the membranes to create segments of grapefruit.

Let the chocolate cakes cool slightly on a wire rack, then transfer to dessert plates and serve warm with grapefruit segments and vegan vanilla ice cream, if desired.

MAKES 8 LITTLE CAKES

Preparation time
30 minutes + 20 minutes baking time

Kitchen equipment
Hand mixer or stand mixer, 8 mini cake pans

Ingredients
· 1 cup (120 g) tiger nut flour
· ⅓ cup (40 g) cornstarch
· 2 tsp baking powder
· 1 pinch salt
· 7 ounces (200 g) dark chocolate
· 4 tbsp olive oil + more to grease the cake cases
· ⅓ cup (80 ml) plant-based milk
· 1 grapefruit
· optional: vegan vanilla ice cream

COCONUT AND CARDAMOM MOUSSE WITH MELON

ALMOND · VANILLA · COFFEE BRITTLE

SERVES 4 TO 8

Preparation time
1 hour + overnight chilling

Kitchen equipment
Hand mixer or stand mixer, freestanding or immersion blender

For the mousse
· ⅔ cup (150 ml) aquafaba (chickpea water; from 1 can of chickpeas)
· 1 ¾ ounces (50 g) coconut butter (creamed coconut)
· 3 tbsp coconut oil
· 1 ¾ ounces (50 g) cocoa butter
· ¾ cup (200 g) soy yogurt
· 7 ounces (200 g) silken tofu
· ¼ cup (50 g) blanched almond butter (or macadamia nut butter)
· 1 tsp ground cardamom
· 1 pinch bourbon vanilla powder
· 1 pinch salt
· 2 ¼ tbsp agave syrup
· 2 tsp locust bean gum (carob bean gum)

For the coffee brittle
· 1 ¾ ounces (50 g) coffee beans
· ¼ cup (50 g) white cane sugar
· ½ tsp ground cinnamon

For the melon
· 1 cantaloupe
· 1 pinch bourbon vanilla powder
· some lemon zest

Whisk the chickpea water in a large bowl until stiff. Melt the coconut butter, coconut oil, and cocoa butter in a bowl suspended over a pan of simmering water.

Blend the yogurt, tofu, and almond butter until very smooth. Add the cardamom, vanilla powder, and salt. Sweeten with agave syrup to taste, then add the melted coconut and cocoa butter mixture and stir until well combined. Stir in the locust bean gum. Transfer to a large bowl, carefully fold in the whisked aquafaba, and chill in the refrigerator overnight.

To prepare for making the coffee brittle, line a large plate with parchment paper. Roughly chop the coffee beans (or grind them with a pestle and mortar). Heat the white cane sugar in a medium nonstick pan over moderate to high heat. As soon as the sugar begins to melt (at first it will melt slowly, but this soon speeds up), add the coffee beans and cinnamon. Continue heating, stirring constantly, until the liquid sugar has coated the beans and is turning slightly brown. Tip the mixture out onto the lined plate and spread out thinly. After about 10 minutes, the brittle will be firm and can be broken into pieces.

Slice the cantaloupe in half and remove and discard the seeds. Remove the flesh from the skin then chop into small cubes. In a medium bowl, mix the cubes of melon with the vanilla powder and lemon zest. Divide the melon between glasses or small bowls, top each with a scoop of mousse, and serve garnished with pieces of coffee brittle.

FROZEN CASHEW CUBES

BERRIES · DATE · ALMOND · COCONUT

MAKES 16 CUBES

Preparation time
50 minutes + overnight soaking
+ overnight chilling

Kitchen equipment
Food processor or immersion
blender, roughly 10 x 10-inch
(25 × 25 cm) freezer-proof dish

Recipe photo see p. 136/137

Grind the almonds, coconut flakes, oats, pitted dates, and salt in a food processor until crumbly. Line the freezer-proof dish with parchment paper, spread the mixture evenly into the bottom of the dish, and press down firmly.

For the cashew cream, melt the coconut butter and cocoa butter in a bowl suspended over a pan of simmering water. Zest and juice the lemon. Drain the cashew pieces in a sieve, rinse with cold water, and blend with the dates, vanilla powder, lemon zest and juice, salt and 1 ½ cups (360 ml) of water. Process everything for several minutes until smooth, light, and creamy. Pour in the warm coconut oil and cocoa butter mixture and blend briefly until well combined. Stir in the locust bean gum.

Transfer half of the cashew cream to the freezer-safe dish and spread evenly over the nut base. Press the berries into the mixture, then spread the rest of the cashew cream on top. Cover and freeze overnight.

Before serving, let the frozen mixture defrost slightly, then slice into 16 cubes using a large knife.

Quick and easy: Frozen cube variations

*These frozen cubes are an incredibly easy, refreshing dessert,
and also very easy to adapt.*

Purple/Pink cubes: *The cashew cream can be colored purple with
blueberries, or pink with raspberries. Purée
3 ½ ounces (100 g) of the selected berries with the
cream.*

Golden cubes: *The addition of 3 ½ ounces (100 g) of puréed mango
gives the cashew cream a golden color. Instead
of berries, put chunks of mango or pineapple between the cream layers before freezing.*

Green cubes: *The cashew cream can be given a delicate green
color and an aromatic flavor by puréeing 20 basil
leaves with the other ingredients. Peach halves
make the ideal filling here.*

Peanut butter cubes: *For a peanut butter option, add 1 banana and
2 tbsp of peanut butter to the cream mixture. For
a chocolatey flavor, try adding 2–3 tbsp of cocoa
powder too. Bananas split in half work well as the
fruit layer for this version.*

For the nut base
· ¾ cup (100 g) almonds
· 1 cup (100 g) unsweetened coconut
  flakes
· 1 ¼ cups (110 g) (gluten-free) oats
· 3 ½ ounces (100 g) Medjool dates,
  pitted
· 1 pinch salt

For the cashew cream
· 3 ½ ounces (100 g) coconut butter
  (creamed coconut)
· 1 ¾ ounces (50 g) cocoa butter
· 1 lemon
· 10 ½ ounces (300 g) cashew
  pieces (or whole cashews), soaked
  in water overnight
· 3 ½ ounces (100 g) Medjool dates,
  pitted
· ½ tsp bourbon vanilla powder
· 1 pinch salt
· 2 tsp locust bean gum (carob bean
  gum)

Also
· 14 ounces (400 g) fresh berries
  (such as strawberries, raspberries,
  or blueberries)

AUTUMN

The chilly evenings, the wisps of morning mist over the countryside — and the golden October sunshine that magically makes it disperse. Colorful leaves and a wild autumnal wind. This is a season for home comforts. Autumn brings a whole range of scents, colors, and delicate flavors — from sweet, juicy pears to earthy pumpkins and all kinds of mushrooms. Our creativity is fired up by the culinary variety at harvest time and there is endless potential for unique creations.

BIRCHER MUESLI WITH PEAR

NUT MILK · CINNAMON · GINGER

For the Bircher mix, combine the oats, millet flakes, buckwheat flakes, sunflower seeds, pumpkin seeds, flaxseeds, and raisins in a large bowl. Transfer to a large storage jar with a lid.

To make the muesli, put the Bircher mix in a small bowl, cover with water, and leave to soak overnight at room temperature.

When you are ready to eat, roughly grate the pear, removing and discarding the stem and core. Stir the grated fruit into the soaked Bircher mixture. Blend the nut butter and about ⅓ cup (80 ml) of warm water to make a nut milk. If using, add cinnamon, ginger, and salt.

Pour the nut milk over the muesli, stir, and enjoy with your choice of chopped nuts, seeds, and/or dried fruit.

Did you know:
I make large batches of the Bircher mix, so I always have a ready supply. This is a great everyday timesaver, and keeps well if stored in a sealed jar and kept in a cool, dry place.

SERVES 1
+ MAKES 1 VERY GENEROUS JAR OF BIRCHER MIX FOR THE LARDER

Preparation time
20 minutes + overnight soaking

Kitchen equipment
Freestanding or immersion blender

For the Bircher mix
· 2 ¼ cups (200 g) (gluten-free) oats
· 2 cups (200 g) millet flakes (or quinoa flakes)
· 1 ¼ cups (200 g) buckwheat flakes (milled buckwheat groats)
· ¾ cup (100 g) sunflower seeds
· ¾ cup (100 g) pumpkin seeds
· ⅔ cup (100 g) flaxseeds
· ⅔ cup (100 g) raisins

For the muesli
· 1 ¾ ounce (50 g) Bircher mix
· 1 pear (or apple)
· 1 tbsp nut butter (such as cashew or almond)
· optional: ½ tsp ground cinnamon
· optional: ¼ tsp ground ginger
· optional: 1 pinch salt
· optional: whatever nuts, seeds, and dried fruit you feel like adding

NUTCRACKER GRANOLA

OAT · COCONUT · DATE

MAKES 1 VERY LARGE STORAGE JAR OF GRANOLA FOR THE LARDER

Preparation time
20 minutes
+ 45–50 minutes baking time

Ingredients
· 10 ounces (300 g) mixed nuts of your choice
· 7 ounces (200 g) dates, pitted
· ½ cup (120 g) coconut oil
· 5 ¼ cups (500 g) (gluten-free) oats
· ¾ cup (100 g) pumpkin seeds (or other seeds)
· 1 ¼ cups (100 g) unsweetened coconut flakes
· optional: 4 ½ ounces (125 g) puffed amaranth (or puffed millet)
· 5 ½ tbsp maple syrup

Preheat the oven to 200°F (100°C) (convection setting). Roughly chop the nuts and slice the dates into thin strips. Heat the coconut oil in a small saucepan until melted.

Combine the nuts, oats, pumpkin seeds, coconut flakes, and puffed amaranth in a large bowl. In a medium bowl, stir together the melted coconut oil, maple syrup, and about ⅔ cup (150 ml) of water, then add to the dry ingredients. Mix well using your hands until you have a crumbly, sticky mixture. If the mixture seems too dry, work in a bit more water — the granola should clump together slightly.

Line a baking sheet with parchment paper and spread the granola evenly in the lined baking sheet. Bake for 35–40 minutes, stirring every 10 minutes, until lightly golden. Add the dates, stir to incorporate, and bake for an additional 10 minutes until the granola is golden brown all over. Let the granola cool completely then transfer to a jar with a lid, seal, and store in a cool, dry place.

Tip:

The nutcracker granola will keep for at least 4 weeks in an airtight container.

NO!TELLA

HAZELNUT · DATE · COCOA

Heat the cocoa butter in a small saucepan until melted.

Purée the dates with ⅓ to ⅔ cup (80–150 ml) of the soaking water until you have a thick paste. Add the hazelnut butter, cocoa powder, and salt then process until smooth and creamy. Finally, add the melted cocoa butter and plant-based milk and process again.

If you like, add vanilla powder or other spices to the creamy paste. Transfer to a storage jar with a lid and store in a cool place.

MAKES 1 MEDIUM JAR

Preparation time
15 minutes + overnight soaking

Kitchen equipment
Freestanding or immersion blender

Ingredients
· 1 ounce (30 g) cocoa butter
· 3 ½ ounces (100 g) dates, pitted and soaked in water overnight
· ¾ cup (150 g) hazelnut butter
· ¼ cup (30 g) cocoa powder
· 1 pinch salt
· ⅓ cup plus 2 tbsp (100 ml) plant-based milk
· optional: 1 pinch bourbon vanilla powder or other ground spices of your choice

Tip:

A pretty jar of this hazelnut and chocolate spread makes a lovely gift, and it is delicious eaten with a sweet yeast loaf or some banana bread. It will keep for at least 4–5 days if refrigerated in an airtight container — if you can resist eating it for that long.

THE HAZELNUT

Hazelnuts are genuine nuts. Their hard pericarp consists of three layers and completely envelops the nut inside.

The **common hazel** belongs to the birch family and is generally a shrub that has multiple stems and grows to 16 to 20 feet (5 to 6 meters) in height. This is a deciduous plant that loves warm climates. Only rarely does the hazel grow into a tree. For the **hazel bush** to thrive and produce a rich crop, it needs well-ventilated soil that is rich in nutrients and humus. The main variety grown for commercial purposes, along with the common hazel, is **Corylus maxima**.

The hazel is monoecious — in other words, each bush has both female and male inflorescences.

Pollination is done by wind and global warming due to climate change is having a major impact on the flowering period of the hazelnut. Buds often open much earlier now than they would have done 50 years ago.

The **hazelnut** itself is shaped like a bell, sometimes slightly elongated, sometimes bulbous and round. Nutcrackers are required to crack open the hard, woody shell. Inside its brown papery skin, the **hazelnut** itself is a creamy color and almost spherical.

HEALTH BENEFITS

Hazelnuts contain around 60 percent fat, which makes them one of the nuts with the highest fat content. However, this consists mainly of unsaturated fatty acids, which have a positive effect on the metabolism of fat. Hazelnuts have a carbohydrate content of around 11 percent and a protein content of about 12 percent, so they are a good source of protein for people following a vegan diet. Furthermore, it is worth noting hazelnuts' very high levels of vitamin E. These little nuts are also packed with B vitamins and lots of minerals, such as calcium, potassium, and phosphorus.

ECONOMIC CHALLENGES

Hazelnuts are native to Europe and Asia Minor, with major cultivation areas in Turkey, Italy, and France. The plants grown for commercial processing produce quite large, round nuts, which are easier to crack using industrial machinery and can be roasted more evenly.

Although hazelnuts are sometimes cultivated in central Europe, the prevailing climatic conditions preclude a reliable or profitable harvest. By some margin, most of the hazelnuts that are commercially available are grown in Turkey. The nuts for organic, fair trade retail are grown on small-scale plots of land, where they are picked and processed manually. Binding price guarantees have been introduced for top-quality produce, which are not lowered even for large purchase volumes. This safeguards jobs for producers and offers a reliable income, which protects livelihoods.

To meet high demands, nuts for conventional retail are grown in monocultures, where pesticides are often used. It is not unusual for harvesting in Turkey to take place under dubious working conditions, sometimes even using child labor.

Other large exporters dominating the global market include the United States and China, generally not with particularly sustainable production methods. Consequently, when buying hazelnuts, it is very important to seek out fair trade, organically cultivated produce, preferably from Europe.

CULINARY USES

Hazelnuts are frequently used in baking and ground hazelnuts are incorporated in lots of pastries and cake mixes. Life without hazelnut spreads is unthinkable, and a particularly popular option combines the nuts with chocolate. Hazelnuts also have an incredible fragrance, which is particularly intense after roasting, and this is another reason for their popularity in baking. In savory cuisine, they make an indispensable nutty addition to salads, while hazelnut butter adds the perfect finishing touch to marinades and sauces.

Main cultivation areas for hazelnuts

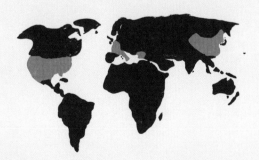

151

SPICED OAT AND HEMP SEED BREAD

WALNUT · MILLET · FENNEL · CARAWAY

FOR 1 LOAF

Preparation time

20 minutes + 8–12 hours soaking time + 1 hour 5 minutes baking time

Kitchen equipment

Food processor, approx. 12 × 4-inch (30 × 10 cm) loaf pan

Ingredients

· 3 ½ ounces (100 g) walnuts
· 2 ounces (60 g) flaxseed meal
· 1 ounce (30 g) hemp seeds
· 2 ¾ cups (240 g) (gluten-free) oats
· ¾ cup (100 g) millet flour (or ragi flour)
· ¾ cup (100 g) buckwheat flour
· 2 ounces (60 g) ground psyllium husks
· 1 tbsp salt
· 1 tsp baking soda
· 1 tsp each fennel seeds, caraway seeds, and aniseeds (or ground fennel, caraway, and aniseed)
· 2–4 tbsp lemon juice (or cider vinegar)

Roughly chop the walnuts if preferred. Grind the flax-seeds and hemp seeds to a fine consistency. Combine the walnuts, flaxseeds, hemp seeds, oats, millet flour, buckwheat flour, psyllium husks, salt, baking soda, fennel, caraway, and aniseed in a large bowl. Add 2 ½ cups (600 ml) of water and the lemon juice and stir with a wooden spoon. The mixture will initially be runny, but it will soon firm up once the psyllium husks and flaxseeds begin to swell.

Line the loaf pan with parchment paper, leaving a 1-inch (2.5 cm) overhang on the long sides. Transfer the bread dough to the pan and smooth the surface. Cover the pan with a kitchen towel and let ferment at room temperature for 8–12 hours to allow the seeds to swell.

Preheat the oven to 350°F (180°C) (convection setting). Bake the bread for about 50 minutes. Carefully lift the bread out of the pan using the parchment paper, set directly on the oven rack, and bake for another 15 minutes to create a crust all over. Remove the bread from the oven and let cool completely on a wire rack before slicing.

PUMPKIN SPREAD WITH BRAZIL NUTS

MIXED NUTS · CUMIN · LEMON

SERVES 4 TO 6

Preparation time
15 minutes
+ 20 minutes cooking time

Kitchen equipment
Freestanding or immersion
blender

Ingredients
· about 14 ounces (400 g) Hokkaido
  squash (or peeled butternut
  squash)
· 3–4 tbsp lemon juice
· 3–4 tbsp olive oil
· 3–4 tbsp blended nut butter (such
  as almond, cashew, and Brazil nut
  butter or almond, cashew, peanut,
  and hazelnut butter)
· 1 tsp ground cumin
· salt
· freshly ground pepper
· optional: ground sweet paprika,
  curry powder, or smoked salt
· 1 ¾ ounces (50 g) Brazil nuts (or
  roasted pumpkin seeds)

Recipe photo see p. 153

Remove any seeds and fibers from the squash then slice into cubes. In a large saucepan, cover the squash with water, and bring to a boil. Reduce the heat to moderate and simmer for about 20 minutes until soft, then drain.

Purée the squash, lemon juice, olive oil, blended nut butter, and cumin until you have a creamy spread. Season with salt and pepper. If using, season with ground paprika, curry powder, or smoked salt.

Chop the Brazil nuts and fold into the spread.

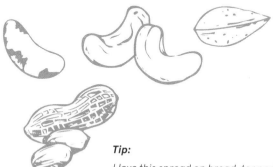

Tip:
I love this spread on bread, topped with lettuce and slices of tofu, or with sliced tempeh and some sprouts.

SMOKY BEAN AND MUSHROOM PÂTÉ

CELERIAC · PARSLEY · MACADAMIA

Peel and dice the celeriac. Clean the button mushrooms and set aside a third of them. Cut the remaining mushrooms into quarters. In a medium saucepan, heat some olive oil and briskly sauté the celeriac and the quartered mushrooms over high heat. Reduce the heat to moderate, cover the pan, and sweat for about 10 minutes, stirring occasionally, until the celeriac and mushrooms are soft.

Put the beans in a sieve and rinse with cold water. Purée the drained beans with the celeriac and mushroom mixture, the macadamia nut butter, smoked salt, tamari, apple syrup, and plenty of pepper until everything is well combined but not quite smooth. If you prefer a smoother pâté, just process it for slightly longer.

Before serving, finely chop the parsley leaves and stems and roughly chop the macadamia nuts. Slice the reserved mushrooms and sauté briskly in some olive oil over high heat until brown. Remove the pan from the heat and season with salt and pepper then add the parsley and macadamia nuts and toss to combine. Serve the pâté with the mushroom, parsley, and macadamia nut topping as a garnish.

Tip:

This pâté makes a wonderful spread for rolls or sandwiches, and it also tastes fantastic with some oven-roasted new potatoes or sweet potato fries.

SERVES 6 TO 8

Preparation time
45 minutes

Kitchen equipment
Freestanding or immersion blender

Ingredients
· 3 ½ ounces (100 g) celeriac
· 10 ounces (300 g) button mushrooms (or oyster mushrooms)
· olive oil
· 7 ounces (200 g) canned or jarred white beans (drained weight)
· ½ cup (100 g) macadamia nut butter
· 1–2 tsp smoked salt
· 2 tbsp tamari soy sauce (strong, dark soy sauce)
· 2 tbsp apple syrup (or agave syrup)
· ground white pepper
· 1 bunch fresh parsley
· ½ cup (65 g) roasted macadamia nuts
· salt

Recipe photo see p. 153

CREAMY CAULIFLOWER AND COCONUT SOUP

TURMERIC FLORET · MISO · MUSTARD SEED

Remove the leaves and the lower part of the stalk from the cauliflower. While keeping the cauliflower whole, separate four large florets, break them into small pieces, and set aside for the topping. Place the whole cauliflower in a large saucepan, add the coconut milk and about ¾ cup (180 ml) of water, and bring to a boil. Cover the pan, reduce the heat to moderate, and simmer for about 20 minutes until the cauliflower is very soft.

Chop the cauliflower into rough chunks in the pan. Add the rice vinegar, miso, chili powder, and ⅓ tsp of salt and blend for 2–3 minutes until thick and creamy. Season with salt, pepper, and possibly more rice vinegar. If you like a hint of sweetness, stir in some agave syrup.

To make the topping, cut four thin slices of lemon and squeeze the juice from the remaining lemon. Heat some coconut oil in a medium pan. Sauté the reserved cauliflower florets with the mustard seeds and turmeric over moderate heat until the florets are soft and turning brown and the mustard seeds begin to pop. Deglaze the pan with the lemon juice, scraping any delicious bits from the bottom of pan.

Divide the cauliflower and coconut soup between deep bowls and garnish each with a slice of lemon and some of the topping.

SERVES 4

Preparation time
30 minutes
+ 20 minutes cooking time

Kitchen equipment
Freestanding or immersion blender

For the soup
· 1 medium cauliflower
· 1 ¾ cups (420 ml) coconut milk
· 3–4 tbsp rice vinegar
· 1 tbsp light miso (shiro miso or lupin miso)
· 1 pinch green chili powder (or green curry paste)
· salt
· freshly ground pepper
· optional: 1–2 tbsp agave syrup (or maple syrup)

For the topping
· ½ lemon
· coconut oil
· 2 tsp mustard seeds
· 1 tsp ground turmeric

Tastes great with:
Freshly baked bread.

Tip:
The cauliflower leaves can be used to make a salad. Slice the leaves diagonally into thin slices then toss in a nutty salad dressing (basic recipe see p. 30).

MILLET COUSCOUS WITH TAHINI AND LEMON DIP

GOLDEN BEET · DATE · CASHEW

SERVES 4

Preparation time
1 hour

Kitchen equipment
Freestanding or immersion blender

For the millet couscous
· 1 cup (200 g) millet (or 1 ½ cups / 300 g couscous)
· salt
· 2 tbsp sesame seeds
· 1 tbsp cumin seeds
· 3 ½ ounces (100 g) cashews
· 3 ½ ounces (100 g) dates, pitted
· 1–2 fresh mild chiles
· 1 bunch fresh basil
· 8 golden beets (or kohlrabi or carrots; about 1 ¼ pounds / 600 g)
· olive oil
· 2 tbsp tamari soy sauce (strong, dark soy sauce)
· 1–2 tbsp date syrup (or agave syrup)

For the tahini and lemon dip
· 1 lemon
· ½ cup (130 g) soy yogurt
· ⅔ cup (160 g) light tahini
· salt

Place the millet in a sieve and rinse under hot running water. Cook in salted water in a saucepan according to the package instructions until the grains swell.

Meanwhile, toast the sesame seeds in a dry pan over moderate heat just until they begin to change color. Add the cumin and continue toasting until fragrant. Remove from the pan and set aside. In the same pan, toast the cashews over moderate heat until golden all over. Slice the dates into thin strips. Slice the chiles into thin rings, removing the seeds if preferred. Strip the basil leaves from the stems. Set the cashews, dates, chiles, and basil aside.

For the dip, grate the lemon zest and roughly chop the flesh of the lemon. Purée the soy yogurt, lemon zest, chopped lemon, tahini, and ⅓ cup (80 ml) of water until light and creamy. Season with salt, transfer to a small bowl, and refrigerate.

Remove any blemishes from the golden beets and slice into large cubes. Heat some olive oil in a medium pan. Sauté the beets briskly over high heat, turning, until light brown on all sides. Reduce the heat to moderate, cover the pan, and continue cooking for about 10 minutes. Deglaze the pan with the tamari and date syrup, scraping any delicious bits from the bottom of the pan. Add the chile rings, mix well, and continue cooking for another 5 minutes.

Transfer the cooked millet to a large bowl and fluff the grains with a fork. Stir in the cumin, sesame seeds, cashews, sliced dates, and basil. Arrange the golden beet and chile mixture over the millet couscous, season with salt, and drizzle generously with olive oil. Drizzle more olive oil over the tahini and lemon dip and serve with the millet.

BAKED RATATOUILLE WITH SALTED ALMONDS

EGGPLANT · BELL PEPPER · OLIVE · HERBS

Preheat the oven to 250°F (120°C). Line a baking sheet with parchment paper. Moisten the almonds slightly with water in a small bowl, sprinkle with the salt and paprika, and mix well to coat. Transfer the almonds to the lined baking sheet and bake for about 25 minutes.

Meanwhile, trim the vegetables and chop into chunks. Remove the leaves from the herbs and roughly chop. Transfer the vegetables, olives, and fresh herbs to a large bowl. Drizzle generously with olive oil, season lightly with salt and pepper, and mix well. Spread the vegetable mixture out in a deep baking pan.

Remove the almonds from the oven and let cool. Increase the oven temperature to 350°F (180°C) and roast the vegetables for 20–30 minutes — make sure the eggplant is well cooked and soft. Let the vegetables cool slightly.

Meanwhile, roughly chop the almonds. Arrange the oven-roasted ratatouille in a shallow bowl, drizzle with balsamic vinegar, sprinkle with fleur de sel and Kampot pepper, and serve scattered with salted almonds.

SERVES 4

Preparation time
30 minutes
+ 20–30 minutes cooking time

Ingredients
· 3 ounces (90 g) almonds
· 1 tsp salt
· ½ tsp smoked paprika (such as Pimentón de la Vera)
· 2 ¼ pounds (1 kg) mixed ratatouille vegetables (zucchini, eggplant, bell peppers, fennel, and tomatoes)
· a couple sprigs each fresh rosemary, thyme, and oregano
· 3 ½ ounces (100 g) green olives, pitted
· olive oil
· freshly ground pepper
· 5 tbsp high-quality mature balsamic vinegar
· fleur de sel
· coarsely ground black Kampot pepper (or freshly ground black pepper)

Tastes great with:
Freshly baked bread, baked potatoes, and an autumnal green salad.

THE
ALMOND

Almonds are not strictly nuts but a type of stone fruit, belonging to the Rosaceae family.

The sparsely leafed **almond tree** is deciduous and grows 10 and 26 feet (3 to 8 meters) high. This undemanding plant has white or pink blossoms and favors a Mediterranean climate and sunny slopes at an altitude of between 2,300 to 5,500 feet (700 to 1700 meters).

Almonds come in three varieties: sweet, soft-shell, and bitter. The latter are toxic, even in small quantities, and cannot be eaten raw. This variety is used to extract bitter almond oil, which is used to flavor liqueurs or marzipan. The most common variety is the **sweet almond**.

Each **almond** is the kernel of a fruit that is similar to the apricot. The layer of fruit surrounding the kernel is thin and has a leathery, dry texture when ripe. Once ripe, the fruit splits open and releases the woody seed inside. This edible seed has a tapered, oval shape and is flattish or slightly bulbous, and covered in a thin, brown skin.

HEALTH BENEFITS

Almonds are an alkaline food with a positive effect on our metabolism and offer plenty of plant-based protein (about 20 percent), which is why they are particularly popular in meat-free cuisine. They are also an excellent source of potassium, calcium, and magnesium, plus copper, folic acid, B vitamins, and vitamin E. Although almonds contain at least 50 percent fat, they supply a lot of unsaturated fatty acids and offer a healthy fatty acid ratio. This means they can have a favorable effect on the cardiovascular system and on cholesterol levels. Because almonds are so easily digestible, they are also popular in food for young children, such as in the form of nut butter in porridge with grains and fruits.

ECONOMIC CHALLENGES

Although almonds are also cultivated in warmer, central European wine-growing regions, the climatic conditions in these areas mean they cannot produce the kinds of yields that are possible in more southerly countries. Wild almond trees thrive particularly well along the eastern Mediterranean coast, in the United States, the Caucasus region, Iraq, Iran, and Pakistan. Commercial plantations are found primarily in California, Spain, Iran, Turkey, Australia, and Morocco.

In addition to warmth and sunlight, almonds, particularly on plantations, need lots of water. Older almond varieties can survive with far lower irrigation levels and have long since thrived in drier regions. The risk of exploiting natural resources is especially high in dry, sunny areas, where cultivated almond trees are supplied with huge amounts of water that would otherwise be used for drinking, and entire bee colonies are driven to plantations to pollinate the plants. This is particularly true in California.

As consumers, we can all support more sustainable farming methods, for example by avoiding conventional almond milk and using oat milk or spelt milk instead, and by shopping for organic, fair trade almonds.

CULINARY USES

Almonds are often found in desserts and especially Christmas baking. But these sweet and exquisitely crunchy nuts have many more uses. Roasted, chopped, and flavored with spices, they add the perfect finishing touch to all sorts of veggie dishes.

Almond butter is a great addition to various salad dressings and blends beautifully with cruciferous vegetables in creamy soups. You can choose between natural almond nut butter with its roasted, nutty, and slightly bitter flavor, or the white variety, made from blanched, peeled nuts, which is slightly sweeter and has hints of marzipan.

Main cultivation areas for almonds

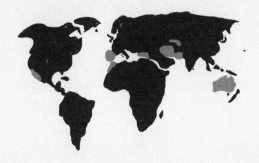

165

ROASTED BEETS WITH LENTIL AND APPLE SALAD

BRAZIL NUT · CILANTRO · LEMON & CASHEW DRESSING

SERVES 4

Preparation time
1 hour

Ingredients
· 7 ounces (200 g) beluga lentils
· 2 beets
· 5 tbsp olive oil
· salt
· 2 tart, crisp apples (such as
  Granny Smith or Honeycrisp)
· 1 bunch fresh cilantro
· ¾ ounce (20 g) salted roasted
  Brazil nuts

For the dressing
· 1 lemon
· 5 tbsp apple cider vinegar
· 3–4 tbsp apple syrup (or maple
  syrup)
· 2 tbsp cashew butter
· ½ tsp salt
· freshly ground pepper

Put the beluga lentils in a sieve and rinse with water. Cook according to the package instructions then drain in a sieve, rinse with cold water, and leave to drain again.

Meanwhile, preheat the oven to 350°F (180°C) (convection setting). Trim the ends off the beets, cut in half, and then cut into thin slices. Toss the sliced beets with the olive oil and some salt in a medium bowl. Spread out on a baking sheet and bake for 15 minutes. Turn the oven to broil or increase the temperature to 500°F (260°C) and cook the beets for another 5–8 minutes.

Meanwhile, quarter and core the apples and chop into fine matchsticks. Roughly chop the cilantro, including the stems. Roughly chop the Brazil nuts.

Zest and squeeze the lemon for the dressing. In a large bowl, combine the lemon juice with the apple cider vinegar, apple syrup, cashew butter, salt, and pepper to make a creamy dressing.

Add the lentils and roasted beets to the dressing and toss to coat. Fold in the apple matchsticks, cilantro, and lemon zest. Season with pepper and possibly more salt. Serve the salad on plates scattered with chopped Brazil nuts.

OVEN-BAKED POTATO SALAD WITH CASHEW SOUR CREAM

DILL · MUSTARD SEED · LEMON

Preheat the oven to 400°F (200°C) (convection setting). Halve or quarter the potatoes and spread them out on a baking sheet. Drizzle the canola oil over the potatoes, season with salt, and toss by hand. Bake for about 25 minutes until starting to brown.

Meanwhile, prepare the cashew sour cream and the dressing. Roughly crumble the tofu for the sour cream. Zest and juice the lemon. Purée the crumbled and silken tofu with the lemon zest and juice for 1–2 minutes until smooth, light, and creamy. Add the cashew butter, purée again, and season with salt and kala namak. Transfer to a medium bowl and refrigerate.

Blend the yogurt, canola oil, apple cider vinegar, maple syrup, and mustard until you have a creamy dressing. (Alternatively, put the ingredients in a medium bowl and stir well to combine).

Toast the mustard seeds in a small dry pan over moderate heat. As soon as they begin to pop, remove the pan from the heat. Put the cooked potatoes in a large bowl and sprinkle immediately with the mustard seeds. Pour the dressing over the potatoes and toss well. Roughly chop the dill and fold into the potatoes. Serve the potato salad with the cashew sour cream.

Tastes great with:
Fried mushrooms and an autumnal green salad.

SERVES 4

Preparation time
40 minutes

Kitchen equipment
Freestanding or immersion blender

For the oven-baked potatoes
· 2 ¼ pounds (1 kg) multicolored new potatoes
· 2–3 tbsp canola oil
· 1 tsp salt

For the cashew sour cream
· 7 ounces (200 g) firm tofu
· ½ lemon
· 14 ounces (400 g) silken tofu
· ½ cup (100 g) cashew butter
· salt
· kala namak (Himalayan black salt, available from well-stocked health food stores or online retailers)

For the dressing
· ½ cup (130 g) plant-based yogurt
· ⅓ cup (80 ml) canola oil (or olive oil)
· ⅓ cup (80 ml) apple cider vinegar (or white balsamic vinegar)
· 2–3 tbsp maple syrup (or agave syrup)
· 2 tsp spicy mustard

Also
· 1 tsp yellow or black mustard seeds
· 1 bunch fresh dill

DECONSTRUCTED LASAGNA WITH SQUASH AND LENTILS

PEAR · GINGER · TURMERIC · CASHEW BÉCHAMEL

SERVES 4

Preparation time
  1 hour 30 minutes

Recipe photo see p. 170/171

For the squash dal, finely chop the ginger and turmeric and slice the chiles into thin rings, removing the seeds if preferred. Halve the squash, remove the seeds and fibers, and slice one half into small cubes. Set the other half aside. Heat some coconut oil in a large saucepan until melted. Add the ginger, turmeric, chiles, fenugreek seeds, aniseeds, and fennel seeds, and sauté over moderate heat for about 2 minutes. Add the diced squash and the lentils and continue cooking, stirring constantly, for 2–3 minutes. Pour in about 2 cups (480 ml) of water and quickly bring to a boil. Cover the pan, reduce the heat to low, and simmer for about 25 minutes. Season with salt and pepper.

Preheat the oven to 350°F (180°C) (convection setting). Line a baking sheet with parchment paper. Slice the second half of the squash into thin wedges and spread out on the lined baking sheet. Brush the squash very lightly with olive oil, lightly season with salt, and bake for about 25 minutes until golden brown.

Meanwhile, for the cashew béchamel, use a balloon whisk to combine the cashew butter, turmeric, nutmeg, and ⅓ cup (80 ml) of hot water in a small bowl. Season with salt and set aside.

For the crunchy cashews, chop the nuts and toast in a small dry pan over moderate heat until golden brown. Sprinkle with curry powder, add the agave syrup, and let caramelize slightly. Remove from the heat and set aside until ready to assemble the lasagna.

Bring a large saucepan of salted water to a boil and cook the sheets of lasagna, occasionally stirring gently to prevent sticking, until al dente. Drain the lasagna sheets in a colander and drizzle with olive oil to prevent sticking.

Halve the pear(s), remove the core(s), and slice very thinly.

To assemble the lasagna, place 1 sheet of pasta on each of four plates. Spread some squash dal evenly on top, drizzle with some of the cashew béchamel, top with roasted squash and sliced pear, and sprinkle with crunchy cashews. Place another sheet of lasagna on top of each serving and repeat these steps until you have created four little towers of lasagna for serving.

Tip:

Of course, you can also bake this lasagna the traditional way in the oven. In this case, make the dal with an additional 2 cups (480 ml) of water so it is runnier, and layer the raw squash wedges and sliced pear with the dal and béchamel between the lasagna sheets. Bake for about 35 minutes in a preheated 350°F (180°C) oven. This lasagna — traditional or deconstructed — tastes fabulous with a green salad or some spicy chutney.

For the squash dal
· 1 piece ginger, roughly 1 ½ to 2-inches (4–5 cm)
· 1 piece turmeric, roughly 1 ½ to 2-inches (4–5 cm)
· 1–2 fresh chiles
· 1 Hokkaido squash (or peeled butternut squash)
· coconut oil (or other vegetable oil)
· 1 tsp each fenugreek seeds, aniseeds, and fennel seeds
· 1 cup (200 g) red lentils
· salt
· freshly ground pepper

For the cashew béchamel
· ½ cup (100 g) cashew butter
· 1 pinch ground turmeric
· 1 pinch ground nutmeg
· salt

For the crunchy cashews
· 3 ½ ounces (100 g) cashews
· ½ tsp curry powder
· 2 ¼ tbsp agave syrup (or maple syrup)

Also
· olive oil
· 16 dried lasagna sheets
· 1–2 ripe but crisp pear(s)

BUCKWHEAT AND MUSHROOM RISOTTO

MISO & ALMOND CREAM · PARSLEY · SALTED ALMOND

Preheat the oven to 250°F (120°C). Line a baking sheet with parchment paper. Moisten the almonds slightly with water in a small bowl, sprinkle with the salt and paprika, and mix well to coat. Transfer the almonds to the lined baking sheet and bake for about 25 minutes.

For the risotto, put the buckwheat in a sieve and rinse under hot running water. Heat 2 tbsp of the olive oil in a large saucepan. Sauté the buckwheat briefly over moderate heat. Add the paprika, season with salt, and then deglaze the pan with some white wine, scraping any delicious bits from the bottom of the pan. Simmer, stirring constantly, until the liquid has been absorbed, then add about 2 cups (480 ml) of water and return to a boil. Cover the pan, reduce the heat to low, and cook until all the liquid has been absorbed. Remove from the heat.

Meanwhile, peel and dice the onion and garlic and trim and slice the mushrooms. Separate the leaves and stems of the parsley, finely chop both, and then set the leaves aside. Heat the remaining 4 tbsp of oil in a large pan. Briskly sauté the onion, garlic, mushrooms, and parsley stems over high heat, and then sweat over moderate heat until the onions and mushrooms are browning nicely.

Combine the almond butter, miso, cornstarch, salt, and ¾ cup (180 ml) of water to make the miso and almond cream. Use this liquid to deglaze the mushroom pan, scraping any delicious bits from the bottom of the pan, then quickly bring to a boil so the sauce thickens slightly.

Roughly chop the salted almonds. Fold half of the creamy mushroom sauce into the buckwheat and season with salt and pepper. Arrange the buckwheat risotto on plates, drizzle with the rest of the sauce, and serve sprinkled with the salted almonds and parsley leaves.

SERVES 4

Preparation time
  1 hour

For the salted almonds
· 3 ounces (90 g) almonds
· 1 tsp salt
· ½ tsp smoked paprika (such as Pimentón de la Vera)

For the buckwheat risotto
· 1 ¾ cups (300 g) buckwheat groats
· 6 tbsp olive oil
· 1 pinch smoked paprika (such as Pimentón de la Vera)
· salt
· Dry white wine (or water)
· 1 red onion
· 1 garlic clove
· 1 ¾ pounds (800 g) mushrooms (such as button, oyster, king oyster, or chanterelles)
· 1 bunch fresh parsley
· freshly ground pepper

For the miso & almond cream
· ¼ cup (50 g) almond butter
· 3 tbsp light miso (shiro miso or lupin miso)
· 4 tsp cornstarch
· 1 pinch salt

SWEET POTATO KUMPIR WITH CASHEW AND MISO QUARK

MÂCHE · ORANGE · WALNUT · GARLIC

SERVES 4

Preparation time

50 minutes (+ overnight soaking + 8–12 hours fermentation time for the cashew quark)

Kitchen equipment

Freestanding blender

For the potatoes

· 4 tsp coarse salt
· 4 large sweet potatoes (each about 10 ounces / 300 g)

For the quark

· 1 garlic clove
· 14 ounces (400 g) cashew quark (basic recipe see p. 25)
· 4 tbsp apple cider vinegar (or a mild white wine vinegar)
· 3 tbsp light miso (shiro miso or lupin miso)
· 1 generous pinch salt

For the salad

· 2 oranges
· 3 ½ ounces (100 g) walnuts
· 14 ounces (400 g) lamb's lettuce

For the dressing

· 5 tbsp walnut oil
· 5 tbsp balsamic vinegar
· 3–4 tbsp maple syrup
· 1 tsp spicy mustard
· ½ tsp salt
· freshly ground pepper

Preheat the oven to 350°F (180°C) (convection setting). Line a baking sheet with parchment paper. Put the coarse salt in a bowl. Wash the sweet potatoes and while they are still wet toss in the salt and then transfer to the lined baking sheet. Bake for 35–40 minutes until tender when pierced with a fork.

Meanwhile, peel and finely chop the garlic. Put the cashew quark in a medium bowl and stir in the garlic, vinegar, miso, and salt.

Segment the oranges. To do this, peel the oranges, removing all the white pith. Working over a bowl to catch the juice, cut between the membranes to create segments of orange. Keep the juice and segments separate.

Toast the walnuts in a small dry pan over moderate heat then set aside.

For the salad dressing, blend the orange juice you collected with the walnut oil, balsamic vinegar, maple syrup, mustard, salt, pepper, and about 3 tbsp of water. (Alternatively, stir the ingredients together in a small bowl). Put the lamb's lettuce in a large bowl and mix in the orange segments. Drizzle the dressing over the salad and toss well.

Put 1 baked sweet potato on each plate, slice lengthwise in half, and then fluff up the inside slightly. Spread some of the cashew and miso quark on each sweet potato. Arrange a portion of salad in or alongside each potato and serve immediately, scattered with roasted walnuts.

NUTTY MEATBALLS WITH A CASHEW SAUCE

BEET · CAPER · LEMON

**SERVES 4
(ROUGHLY 16–24 MEATBALLS)**

Preparation time
1 hour 15 minutes
+ 20 minutes resting time

Kitchen equipment
Freestanding blender or spice grinder, hand mixer or stand mixer

For the marinated beets
· 7 ounces (200 g) cooked beets
· 4 tbsp mild white wine vinegar (or white balsamic vinegar)
· 4 tbsp olive oil
· 1 tsp agave syrup
· 1 tsp spicy mustard
· ½ tsp salt
· freshly ground pepper

Recipe photo see p. 178/179

To make the marinated beets, slice the beets into roughly ⅓-inch (1-cm) cubes and put in a small bowl. Shake the white wine vinegar, olive oil, agave syrup, mustard, salt, and pepper in a jar with a lid to make the marinade. (Alternatively, stir the ingredients together in a small bowl.) Drizzle over the beets and set aside.

For the meatballs, stir the psyllium husks into ½ cup (120 ml) of water in a small bowl and leave to swell for about 10 minutes.

Meanwhile, crumble the tofu into a large bowl. Peel and very finely dice the onion. Grind the cashews and Brazil nuts until crumbly — don't worry if a few larger pieces remain. Add the ground nuts, onion, yeast flakes, nori flakes, tamari, flaxseed oil, liquid smoke, salt, and pepper to the crumbled tofu and mix well. Add the chestnut flour and the soaked psyllium husks, then work the mixture using the dough hook attachment until firm enough to be shaped into balls. Leave to rest for about 20 minutes. Finally, shape the mixture by hand into 16–24 little balls.

For the broth, peel the onion and slice into rings. Transfer to a large saucepan, add the peppercorns, allspice berries, bay leaves, and 4 ¼ cups (1 liter) of water and bring to a boil. Reduce the heat so that the water is gently simmering. Add the meatballs and simmer for 15–20 minutes until they float to the surface.

Meanwhile, for the cashew sauce, use a balloon whisk to combine the cashew butter and 1 ⅔ cups (400 ml) of water in a medium saucepan. Add with the nutmeg, salt, and pepper and bring to a boil. Stir the tapioca starch into a small amount of water in a small bowl until smooth, then stir this paste into the cashew sauce and cook until it thickens slightly. Add the capers and season with some lemon juice.

Lift the cooked meatballs out of the broth and serve with the cashew sauce and the marinated beets alongside.

Tastes great with:
Baked or mashed potatoes.

For the meatballs
· 1 ounce (30 g) ground psyllium husks
· 7 ounces (200 g) smoked tofu
· 1 onion
· 3 ½ ounces (100 g) cashew pieces (or whole cashews)
· 3 ½ ounces (100 g) Brazil nuts
· ⅔ cup (40 g) nutritional yeast flakes
· 2 tbsp nori flakes (available from Asian supermarkets or health food stores)
· 4 tbsp tamari soy sauce (strong, dark soy sauce)
· 2 tbsp flaxseed oil
· 1 tbsp liquid smoke (or 1 tsp smoked paprika)
· 1 tsp salt
· freshly ground pepper
· ½ cup (50 g) chestnut flour

For the broth
· 1 onion
· 1 tsp peppercorns
· 2 allspice berries
· 2 bay leaves

For the cashew sauce
· ½ cup (100 g) cashew butter
· ½ tsp ground nutmeg
· 1 pinch salt
· freshly ground pepper
· 4 tsp tapioca flour (or cornstarch)
· 2–3 tbsp capers
· 2–3 tbsp lemon juice

SWEET BEET RAWIOLI

CASHEW · VANILLA · PUMPKIN SEED · POMEGRANATE

SERVES 4

Preparation time
45 minutes + overnight soaking
+ 6–8 hours cooling time

Kitchen equipment
Freestanding or immersion blender

For the cashew and vanilla cream
· 2 ounces (60 g) coconut oil (or
  1 ounce / 30 g each coconut oil
  and cocoa butter)
· 5 ¼ ounces (150 g) cashew pieces
  (or whole cashews), soaked in
  water overnight
· 4 dates, pitted and soaked in
  water overnight
· ½ tsp bourbon vanilla powder (or
  pure vanilla extract)
· 2–3 tbsp coconut flour

Also
· ¾ cup (100 g) pumpkin seeds
· 2 tbsp white cane sugar
· 4 tbsp maple syrup
· 2 large beets
· 1 pomegranate
· pumpkin seed oil

Tip:
You will only need 24–32 thin slices of
beet for the ravioli. The rest of the beets
can be used in a soup (recipe see p.
52/53) or salad (recipe see p. 166).

For the cashew and vanilla cream, heat the coconut oil in a small saucepan until melted.

Drain the cashews in a sieve and rinse with cold water. Remove the dates from their soaking liquid, reserving the liquid, and purée with the cashews and vanilla powder until thick. Measure the reserved date soaking liquid and add enough water to come ⅓ to ⅔ cup (80 to 150 ml) total. Add to the date mixture and blend until you have a thick cream that is similar to cream cheese in consistency. Continue processing on low for another 20–30 seconds while adding the melted coconut oil, followed by the coconut flour — the coconut flour will bind the cream together and how much you need depends on how much liquid you. Transfer to a medium bowl and refrigerate for 6–8 hours.

Line a plate with parchment paper. Briefly toast the pumpkin seeds in a small dry pan over moderate heat. Add the white cane sugar and maple syrup and let caramelize, stirring constantly with a wooden spoon. Spread the seeds on the lined plate and let cool.

Remove the root ends on the beets and then cut them in half. Use a peeler to cut a total of 24–32 very thin slices from the cut sides of the beets (reserve the ends for another use; see tip). Cut the pomegranate in half and scoop out the seeds.

Arrange 3–4 beet slices next to each other on each of four plates. Top each slice with a walnut-sized portion of the cashew and vanilla cream, cover with another slice of beet, and press down gently around the sides. Drizzle the sweet beet ravioli with pumpkin seed oil and serve scattered with caramelized pumpkin seeds and pomegranate seeds.

THE COCONUT

The coconut is a stone fruit and not a genuine nut. It is the fruit of the coconut palm and is harvested all year-round.

Sturdy, evergreen **coconut palms** grow to almost 100 feet (30 meters) in height and need plenty of light, tropical warmth, and loose, sandy, nutrient-rich soil. They require huge amounts of water and thrive in regions with high levels of precipitation. The palms reach peak capacity when they are about 12 years old, producing 30 to 40 coconuts each year.

For people living in tropical coastal regions, coconut palms have always been an excellent natural resource. Coconuts are a nourishing form of food, plus wood from the trees can be used to build huts and the palm leaves can be used for roofing. The fibers are woven to create wall materials, baskets, and ropes, while the dry coconut shells can be burned for fuel.

The inside of the fibrous, hard shell of the **coconut** is coated with ⅓ to ¾ inch (1 to 2 cm) of thick white fruit flesh and the coconut water is held in the central hollow area inside the flesh. Drinking coconuts are harvested when they are still green; they contain lots of water, but the flesh of the fruit is less well developed. Coconuts intended for eating are left to mature for longer. During this process, they lose water, and form a thicker white flesh layer and a harder shell.

Ripe coconuts are harvested using knives attached to long poles or by expert coconut palm climbers. In Malaysia, Thailand, and Indonesia they even use little monkeys that have been trained to fetch the fruit from the trees.

Almost all parts of the coconut have their uses: the coconut water, the flesh of the fruit, and the skin. The dried **white flesh (copra)** is used to produce coconut oil and creamed coconut. It can also be used to make coconut milk, flour, chips, and flakes.

As well as being used in cooking and baking, pressed coconut oil has an industrial application in the manufacture of cosmetics and pharmaceutical products.

HEALTH BENEFITS

The flesh of the coconut contains up to 50 percent water after harvesting and constitutes a staple food in many tropical regions. It consists of about 36 percent fat, so is very high in energy. It also contains lots of dietary fiber, and is a good source of potassium, magnesium, and other micronutrients. Since the fat is mainly made up of less healthy saturated fatty acids, coconuts should only be enjoyed in moderation.

After drying, the water content is about 5 percent and the flesh of the coconut has a shelf life similar to other nuts. The fat content rises to about 65 percent for the dried product.

ECONOMIC CHALLENGES

Coconut oil is booming, particularly since the environmental damage caused by conventional palm oil cultivation has attracted criticism — other than in certified organic plantations, palm oil production continues to cause rainforest destruction. Coconut oil is a welcome alternative because coconut palms do not generally grow in monocultures and even in the main centers of production (Indonesia, the Philippines, and India generate about 91 percent of the global harvest), producers are mostly organized in small farms. Unfortunately, most of these farmers live below the poverty line. It is also important to note that increased demand for coconut oil is resulting in more professional cultivation methods and greater land requirements. For this reason, it is important to look for fair trade coconut oil and other coconut products.

CULINARY USES

Coconut is an incredibly versatile ingredient. Thanks to its high levels of saturated fatty acids, coconut oil can be heated to a high temperature and is wonderful for baking and brisk sautéing. The slightly sweet, subtle coconut flavor is also welcome in raw cuisine. Raw cakes, pralines, and ice cream can all be thickened beautifully with coconut oil or creamed coconut, because they solidify when cold, adding stability to your culinary creations.

Coconut milk is a fabulous alternative to cream and is particularly popular in Asian cuisine. Coconut chips and flakes taste great in muesli, and make a crunchy topping for salads, soups, and curries.

Main cultivation areas for coconut

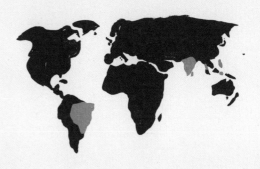

SQUASH AND ALMOND CRÈME BRÛLÉE

COCONUT · VANILLA · TIPSY ORANGE

Remove the seeds and fiber from the squash, then dice the flesh. In a large saucepan, combine the squash with just enough water to cover and bring to a boil. Cover the pan, reduce the heat to moderate, and simmer for about 20 minutes until soft.

Add the coconut butter to the hot squash and cooking liquid and let it melt slightly. Add the salt, vanilla powder, and agave syrup, if using, and blend until creamy and well combined. Add the almond butter and Grand Marnier and combine well, then season with lemon juice to taste — the lemon should not dominate but create a balanced flavor.

While it is still runny, divide the creamy mixture between four dessert dishes and refrigerate for 6–8 hours (or overnight). Before serving, sprinkle each dish with 1 tablespoon of sugar and caramelize the top with the kitchen torch to create a classic caramel crust.

SERVES 4

Preparation time
40 minutes + 20 minutes cooking + 6–8 hours chilling time

Kitchen equipment
Freestanding or immersion blender, kitchen torch

Ingredients
· 1 ¼ pounds (600 g) Hokkaido squash (or peeled butternut squash)
· 1 ounce (30 g) coconut butter (creamed coconut)
· 1 pinch salt
· 1 pinch bourbon vanilla powder
· optional: 2–3 tbsp agave syrup (or white cane sugar)
· ½ cup (100 g) almond butter
· ¼ cup (60 ml) Grand Marnier (or Cointreau)
· 2–3 tbsp lemon juice
· 4 tbsp white cane sugar

Did you know:

If you do not own a kitchen torch, you can caramelize ½ cup (100 g) of white cane sugar in a nonstick pan then pour the liquid caramel quickly over the creamy desserts. Be careful to let it cool slightly before serving.

WINTER

Childhood memories of musty forest floors, damp wood, the first frost, snowflakes, and the incomparable scent of Christmas cookies. At the top of the menu are squash, cabbage, and root vegetables. Hearty and filling food is the order of the day, so we can curl up, satisfied with a good book to read by candlelight, and enjoy the peaceful winter atmosphere.

WARM BREAKFAST RICE WITH COCONUT AND ORANGE

VENERE RICE · GINGER · ALLSPICE

For the rice, heat the coconut oil in a large saucepan. Sauté the ginger and allspice briefly, then add the rice and continue cooking for a few minutes. Add 1 ¼ cups (300 ml) of water and the salt and bring to a boil. Cover the pan, reduce the heat to low, and simmer, stirring occasionally, until all the water has been absorbed.

Meanwhile, for the topping, grate the zest of 1 orange and cut both oranges into segments. To do this, peel the oranges, removing all the white pith. Cut between the membranes to create segments of orange. Slice the ginger crosswise into very thin rounds then cut the rounds into thin strips. Heat the coconut oil in a small pan and sauté the ginger over moderate heat until browned. Add the coconut flakes and let brown slightly then remove from the heat and set aside.

When the rice is fully cooked, remove from the heat, fold in the coconut butter, cover the pan, and let stand for 15 minutes. Stir in the orange zest.

Divide the coconut rice between small bowls, top with the orange segments, sprinkle with the ginger and coconut mixture, and serve warm.

SERVES 4

Preparation time
1 hour

For the rice
· 2 tbsp coconut oil
· 1 pinch ground ginger
· 1 pinch ground allspice
· ½ cup (100 g) Venere black rice (or Nerone black rice)
· 1 pinch salt
· 2 ounces (60 g) coconut butter (creamed coconut)

For the topping
· 2 oranges
· 1 piece ginger, roughly 1 ½ inches (4 cm)
· 1 tbsp coconut oil
· 4 tbsp unsweetened coconut flakes

Did you know:

When segmenting the oranges, it is best to work over a bowl so you can catch the juice. Squeeze what is left of the oranges by hand over the bowl. You can top up the juice with hot water and add a couple slices of fresh ginger for a lovely breakfast drink.

CREAMY POLENTA PORRIDGE WITH CINNAMON PLUMS

ALMOND · CHILI

SERVES 4

Preparation time
40 minutes

For the porridge
· 2 cups (480 ml) almond milk (or another plant-based milk)
· 1 pinch salt
· 1 cup (160 g) coarse polenta
· 2 tbsp almond butter

For the cinnamon plums
· 14 ounces (400 g) canned plums
· 2 tbsp coconut oil (or vegan margarine)
· 1 tsp ground cinnamon
· 1 pinch chili powder
· 1 pinch salt

Also
· 1 ½ ounces (45 g) almonds

Bring the almond milk and salt to a boil in a large saucepan. Pour in the polenta, stirring constantly, and return to a boil. Turn off the heat, cover the pan, and leave to thicken for about 15 minutes.

Meanwhile, drain the plums in a sieve, reserving the liquid. Heat the coconut oil in a small saucepan. Add the plums, cinnamon, chili powder, and salt and cook over moderate heat for about 10 minutes. Occasionally pour in some of the reserved plum liquid to prevent the fruit from burning.

Roughly chop the almonds and toast in a small dry pan over moderate heat. Stir the almond butter into the thickened polenta.

Divide the porridge between small deep dishes, arrange the cinnamon plums on top, scatter with the almonds, and eat warm.

Quick and easy:
Chai with almond milk

Homemade chai with almond milk is the perfect drink for a winter breakfast. Roughly chop a 1-inch (2.5 cm) piece of ginger. Toast ½ tsp each of fennel seeds, aniseeds, peppercorns, cardamom pods, and ground cinnamon, plus 4 cloves, in a large dry pan for 2–3 minutes. Add the ginger and 4 ¼ cups (1 liter) of water and bring to a boil. Reduce the heat to low and simmer for 20 minutes. Remove from the heat, add 1 tbsp of Assam tea, and leave to infuse for 10–15 minutes. Strain through a fine sieve, sweeten with 1 tbsp of raw cane sugar, and serve with warm almond milk (basic recipe see p. 24).

RAW BEET SPREAD

MACADAMIA · CHILE

Roughly chop the macadamia nuts. Remove the root ends of the beets and trim any blemished or fibrous areas. Roughly dice the beets.

Purée the beets with the yeast flakes, olive oil, apple cider vinegar, tamari, and salt until as smooth or chunky as desired. Stir in the agave syrup and season with some chile flakes, pepper, and/or vinegar, if using.

Transfer the beet spread to a bowl, stir in all but 2 tbsp of the macadamia nuts. Serve scattered with the reserved nuts.

SERVES 4 TO 8

Preparation time
20 minutes

Kitchen equipment
Freestanding or immersion blender

Ingredients
· 4 ¼ ounces (120 g) roasted macadamia nuts
· 14 ounces (400 g) beets
· 5 tbsp nutritional yeast flakes
· 5 tbsp olive oil
· 2 tbsp apple cider vinegar
· 2 tbsp tamari soy sauce (strong, dark soy sauce)
· 1 tsp salt
· 1 tbsp agave syrup
· optional: chile flakes, freshly ground pepper, or a splash of vinegar

Tip:
If covered, the spread will keep in the refrigerator for about 6 days and tastes fantastic on bread, served as a dip with potatoes, or as an alternative to pesto with pasta.

THE
MACADAMIA

Macadamias originate from Australia and bear the name "Queen of the nuts." They are one of the most expensive varieties.

The **macadamia tree** belongs to the Proteaceae family and is an evergreen that is very sensitive to the cold, thrives in subtropical, damp climates, and grows to a height of almost 60 feet (18 meters). The trees initially bear fruit after 7 to 10 years and, from then on, can yield up to 110 pounds (50 kilograms) of nuts per year. Only two macadamia varieties are suitable for consumption; the nuts produced by other varieties are inedible.

The lovely round **macadamia nut** consists of two seed halves. Each nut grows separately, dangling on a stalk, and is enclosed in a woody husk, which in turn, is protected by a thick green shell. As soon as macadamia nuts are ripe, the fruits detach and fall to the ground. After the nuts are collected, they are dried and shelled. The green outer layer is used for animal fodder or fertilizer and the hard shells must be cracked manually using special nut crackers to avoid damaging the nut.

HEALTH BENEFITS

With a fat content of about 72 percent, macadamias are among the nuts richest in fat and calories. It is important to note that these are primarily monounsaturated fatty acids, which have a positive impact on cholesterol levels. Macadamia nuts also contain lots of dietary fiber that aids digestion and plenty of minerals and trace elements like potassium, magnesium, iron, B vitamins, and vitamin E.

Incidentally, macadamia nuts are toxic for dogs and cats.

ECONOMIC CHALLENGES

Macadamias originally came from the rainforests in eastern Australia. Even though the trees are somewhat reluctant to grow and require specific soil conditions and climate, they are now cultivated outside Australia, including in Hawaii, which is the largest producer, along with New Zealand, South Africa, Malawi, Kenya, Rwanda, Israel, Brazil, California, Guatemala, Paraguay, and Bolivia.

Due to the challenges of cultivating macadamias — the laborious harvesting technique and complex processing — and the increasing demand, macadamias are some of the most expensive nuts.

Unfortunately, fair trade production and retail are not particularly common for macadamias. The nuts are exported unshelled, with harvesting controlled by foreign landowners, which means many farmers live in poverty and are not self-sufficient. Organic farming is a worthy aspiration for all cultivation regions. Once again, consumer choices can help influence the argument for greater equity and fairness.

CULINARY USES

Macadamia nuts have a mild, slightly sweet flavor and their high fat content gives them a creamy, almost buttery taste. They have not been widely used in western cuisine until recently. When macadamias are roasted, they develop an intense flavor that is absolutely irresistible, especially when combined with vegetables. The oily notes work particularly well in heartier, substantial dishes.

Macadamias are excellent in savory and sweet mousses, or as a topping on muesli or porridge.

Main cultivation areas for macadamias

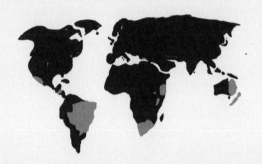

CORN CHOWDER WITH EGGPLANT-WRAPPED DATES

WINTER VEGETABLES · WALNUT · COCONUT

SERVES 4

Preparation time

1 hour 10 minutes + overnight marinating + 20 minutes cooking time

Kitchen equipment

16 toothpicks or 4 long wooden skewers, freestanding or immersion blender

For the dates

· 2 tbsp olive oil
· 2 tbsp tamari soy sauce (strong, dark soy sauce)
· 1 ½ tbsp maple syrup
· 1 pinch smoked paprika (such as Pimentón de la Vera)
· 1 pinch salt
· 1 large eggplant
· 8 Medjool dates
· 16 walnut halves

For the soup

· 2 celery stalks
· 2 garlic cloves
· 1 piece ginger, ¾–1 ½ inches (2–4 cm)
· 10 ounces (300 g) mixed, pale root vegetables (such as parsnips, parsley root, or celeriac)
· 1 ½ pounds (700 g) canned or jarred corn (drained weight)
· ½ lemon
· 2 tbsp coconut oil
· 3 ⅓ cups (800 ml) vegetable broth
· salt
· freshly ground pepper
· chile flakes
· unsweetened coconut flakes
· nigella seeds

For the dates, start one day in advance and stir together the olive oil, tamari, maple syrup, paprika, and salt in a shallow, elongated dish. Remove the stem from the eggplant and slice lengthwise into very thin strips. Slice these strips lengthwise in half. Add the strips of eggplant to the dish and gently flip to coat all over. Cover and leave to infuse for several hours or overnight in the refrigerator.

Preheat the oven to 325°F (160°C) (convection setting). Line a baking sheet with parchment paper. Slice each date in half, remove the stone, and insert 1 walnut half. Wrap each date with 1 marinated strip of eggplant and secure using a toothpick. (Alternatively, slide 4 dates onto 1 long wooden skewer.) Transfer the dates to the lined baking sheet and bake for 20–25 minutes. Remove from the oven, cover, and keep warm.

Meanwhile, for the soup, slice the celery lengthwise in half then dice. Peel and chop the garlic and ginger. Peel and roughly chop the root vegetables. Drain the corn. Zest and juice the lemon.

Heat the coconut oil in a large saucepan. Briskly sauté the celery, garlic, and ginger over high heat. Add the root vegetables and three-quarters of the corn and continue cooking briefly. Add the vegetable broth and bring to a boil. Reduce the heat, cover the pan, and simmer for about 20 minutes until the vegetables are soft. Stir in the lemon zest and a dash of the juice. Purée the chowder until smooth. Season with salt, pepper, chile flakes, and the remaining lemon juice.

Divide the soup between deep bowls, sprinkle with the remaining corn, some chile flakes, coconut flakes, and nigella seeds. Serve with the eggplant-wrapped dates.

CREAMY SQUASH SOUP WITH GARLICKY SPINACH

FENNEL · PUMPKIN SEED · CINNAMON CROUTON

Halve the squash and remove the seeds and fibers. Slice the fennel lengthwise in half then remove and discard the tough base. Chop the squash and fennel into large chunks. Heat some olive oil in a large saucepan. Sauté the fennel seeds and aniseeds over moderate heat until fragrant. Add the squash and fennel, sprinkle with the ginger and turmeric, and sauté briefly and briskly over high heat. Deglaze the pan with the white wine, scraping any delicious bits from the bottom of the pan, then add some water and the salt, cover the pan, and simmer gently over low heat for about 25 minutes until soft.

Meanwhile, cut the bread into cubes to make the cinnamon croutons. Heat some olive oil in a medium pan and toast the bread over moderate to high heat until crisp. Dust the croutons with the cinnamon, add the pumpkin seeds, and continue cooking until the seeds begin to pop. Remove from the pan and set aside.

Heat some more olive oil in the same pan over moderate heat. Peel the garlic, crush with the flat side of a knife, and sauté briefly in the oil. Add the spinach, season with salt and pepper, and cook, stirring constantly, until the leaves are wilted.

Purée the squash, fennel, and any cooking liquid left in the pan for 1–2 minutes until smooth. If the soup is too thick, add some hot water and purée to incorporate. Season with maple syrup, apple cider vinegar, and cayenne pepper.

Divide the soup between four bowls, top with the garlicky spinach, and garnish with the cinnamon croutons and pumpkin seeds.

SERVES 4

Preparation time
1 hour

Kitchen equipment
Freestanding or immersion blender

For the soup
· 2 ¼ pounds (1 kg) Hokkaido squash (or peeled butternut squash)
· 1 fennel bulb
· olive oil
· 1 tsp fennel seeds
· 1 tsp aniseeds
· ½ tsp ground ginger
· ½ tsp ground turmeric
· ⅓ cup (80 ml) white wine (or water)
· 1 tsp salt
· maple syrup
· apple cider vinegar (alternatively, a mild white wine vinegar or lemon juice)
· cayenne pepper

For the cinnamon croutons
· 4 slices (gluten-free) wholegrain or nut bread (such as spiced oat and hemp seed bread, recipe see p. 152)
· olive oil
· ½ tsp ground cinnamon
· 4 tbsp pumpkin seeds

Also
· olive oil
· 2 garlic cloves
· 7 ounces (200 g) baby spinach
· salt
· freshly ground pepper

BEETS WITH CHICKPEAS AND LEMON

BEAN HUMMUS · HORSERADISH · PECAN

SERVES 4

Preparation time
1 hour

Kitchen equipment
Freestanding or immersion blender

For the hummus
· 7 ounces (200 g) canned or jarred white beans (drained weight)
· ½ cup (120 g) tahini
· 5 tbsp lemon juice
· 5 tbsp olive oil
· 1 tsp ground cumin
· 1 tsp salt

Also
· 8 small beets
· 1 lemon
· olive oil
· smoked paprika (such as Pimentón de la Vera)
· salt
· freshly ground pepper
· 7 ounces (200 g) canned or jarred chickpeas (drained weight)
· 1 tsp each cumin seeds, coriander seeds, curry powder, and ground cinnamon
· 1 piece horseradish, 1 to 1 ½ inches (2.5–4 cm)
· 3 ½ ounces (100 g) pecans (or walnuts)
· optional: 1 bunch fresh parsley

For the hummus, put the beans in a sieve and rinse with cold water. Purée the beans with the tahini, lemon juice, olive oil, cumin, and salt until creamy. Set aside.

Preheat the oven to 350°F (180°C) (convection setting). Line a baking sheet with parchment paper. Remove the root ends of the beets and trim any blemished or fibrous areas. Cut each beet into eight wedges and slice the lemon as thinly as possible. Put the beets and lemon in a medium bowl, drizzle with olive oil, season with paprika, salt, and pepper and toss well to coat. Transfer to one half of the lined baking sheet. Reserve the bowl.

Drain the chickpeas in a sieve and rinse with cold water. Transfer to the bowl used for the beets and lemons then add the cumin seeds, coriander seeds, curry powder, cinnamon, and 2 tbsp of olive oil and toss to coat. Spread the chickpeas on the other half of the baking sheet and bake, tossing occasionally to ensure even browning, for 25–35 minutes.

Meanwhile, peel and finely grate the horseradish. Toast the pecans in a small dry pan over moderate heat then chop roughly. Finely chop the parsley, if using.

Transfer the beet and lemon mixture to a bowl, fold in the horseradish and parsley, if using. Spread the hummus on plates and serve with the beet mixture, chickpeas, and pecans.

206

ROASTED BRUSSELS SPROUTS WITH MACADAMIAS

POMEGRANATE · ARUGULA · TAHINI & LEMON SAUCE

Preheat the oven to 350°F (180°C) (convection setting). Line a baking sheet with parchment paper. Heat 3 tbsp of coconut oil in a small saucepan until melted. Clean the Brussels sprouts, slice in half, and spread on the lined baking sheet. Pour the melted coconut oil over the Brussels sprouts, toss to coat all over, and bake for 20–25 minutes until slightly browned.

Meanwhile, cut the pomegranate in half and scoop out the seeds. Roughly chop the arugula leaves. In a small bowl, combine the tahini with 3 tablespoons of the lemon juice and ¾ cup (180 ml) of water to make a creamy sauce. Season lightly with salt.

Heat the remaining coconut oil in a large pan. Sauté the fennel seeds and aniseeds over moderate heat until fragrant. Add the cumin, turmeric, curry powder, and coconut sugar, followed by the roasted Brussels sprouts, and toss to coat. Season with salt, pepper, the remaining lemon juice, and possibly more coconut sugar. Fold in the macadamia nuts.

Transfer the Brussels sprout and macadamia mixture to a serving bowl. Sprinkle with the pomegranate seeds and arugula, drizzle liberally with the tahini and lemon sauce, and serve.

SERVES 4

Preparation time

1 hour

Ingredients

· 4 tbsp coconut oil
· 1 ¾ pounds (800 g) Brussels sprouts
· 1 pomegranate
· 1 bunch arugula leaves
· ½ cup (120 g) tahini
· 4 tbsp lemon juice
· salt
· 1 tsp fennel seeds
· 1 tsp aniseeds
· ½ tsp each ground cumin, ground turmeric, and curry powder
· 2 tsp coconut sugar, plus more if desired
· freshly ground pepper
· 3 ounces (90 g) roasted macadamia nuts

NUT RISSOLES WITH APPLE CARPACCIO

ALMOND · SESAME SEED · ORANGE · JERUSALEM ARTICHOKE

SERVES 4

Preparation time
1 hour 15 minutes

Kitchen equipment
Freestanding or immersion blender

For the carpaccio
· 4 small Jerusalem artichokes
· 1 apple
· ½ orange
· 1 ¾ ounces (50 g) almonds
· 1 tsp mustard seeds
· 4 tbsp flaxseed oil
· 2 tbsp apple cider vinegar
· 1 tbsp maple syrup
· 1 tsp ground cinnamon
· salt

For the nut rissoles
· sesame seeds (or oats)
· 1 ½ cups (150 g) ground almonds
· ½ cup (60 g) lupin flour (or soy flour)
· 2 tbsp ground psyllium husks
· 1 tsp each sweet paprika, smoked paprika, and salt
· 1 tbsp dried thyme
· 1 small onion
· 1–2 celery stalks
· 8 ½ ounces (240 g) canned or jarred kidney beans (drained weight)
· ⅓ cup (20 g) nutritional yeast flakes
· 3 tbsp tamari soy sauce (strong, dark soy sauce)
· 2 tbsp tahini
· olive oil

Remove any blemished sections from the Jerusalem artichokes and slice the bulbs as thinly as possible. Halve and core the apple, then slice as thinly as possible. Zest and juice the orange. Toast the almonds in a small dry pan over moderate heat then chop roughly and set aside. Toast the mustard seeds in the same pan until they begin to pop.

In a large bowl, combine the flaxseed oil, apple cider vinegar, maple syrup, cinnamon, and the orange zest and juice. Season with salt. Add the Jerusalem artichokes, apple, and mustard seeds, toss to coat, and leave to marinate while you make the rissoles.

Scatter a plate with plenty of sesame seeds ready to coat the rissoles. Combine the ground almonds, lupin flour, and psyllium husks in a large bowl. Stir in the sweet paprika, smoked paprika, salt, and thyme. Peel the onion and dice it, along with the celery. Put the kidney beans in a sieve and rinse with cold water. Add the beans, onion, celery, yeast flakes, tamari, and tahini to the dry ingredients and mix well. Purée roughly — don't worry if a few chunks of bean are still visible.

Shape this mixture by hand into 8–12 round flat patties. Roll the rissoles in the sesame seeds to coat. Heat plenty of olive oil in a large pan over moderate heat and fry the rissoles on both sides until crisp.

Divide the Jerusalem artichoke and apple carpaccio between plates, arrange the rissoles on top, and serve scattered with almonds.

Tastes great with:

Dips like the cashew sour cream (recipe see p. 169), hummus (recipe see p. 103), or mashed potatoes.

THE
PISTACHIO

The pistachio — like the cashew — is a stone fruit and belongs to the sumac family.

The **pistachio tree** is a leafy evergreen that can reach a height of almost 40 feet (12 meters) and can live for up to 300 years. The pistachio favors warm, dry, desert-like regions. Since it is a dioecious tree (in other words each tree can only have male or female flowers), it is vital to plant both male and female specimens, so that pollination can take place by wind.

Pistachios grow in clusters — like grapes — on a stalk and can be shaken from the tree when ripe. The stone fruit are usually oval and succulent, with the green, triangular **pistachio kernels**, enveloped by a purple skin and hard shell, beneath.

Harvesting takes place in early autumn, with pistachios being separated from the fleshy fruit in processing facilities before being transferred to large containers of water. The ripe nuts sink to the bottom, while the unripe fruit floats on the surface, allowing them to be skimmed off. Then the drying process starts — either outside in the sun, as would have been traditional in the Middle East, or in special processing units if the nuts are destined for export. As the nuts dry, the shells pop open, making them easy to eat.

HEALTH BENEFITS

Pistachios are popular as a gentle, easily digestible ingredient in therapeutic traditions, such as Ayurvedic and traditional Chinese medicine, and are highly esteemed for the wide range of micronutrients they contain. They are rich in potassium, calcium, magnesium, iron, phosphorus, and zinc, and are a good source of vitamins C and E, plus plenty of B-complex vitamins. These little nuts contain roughly 52 percent fat and 18 percent protein. Like most nuts, they contain lots of unsaturated fatty acids, which are good for fat metabolism and can help prevent cardiovascular disease and arteriosclerosis.

ECONOMIC CHALLENGES

Pistachio cultivation has been documented since antiquity and takes place mainly in the Mediterranean region and Middle East. In the past, pistachios were regarded as a royal delicacy and not something to be consumed by ordinary people. Luckily that is no longer the case today. However, pistachios still command a high price due to widely variable yields and the laborious processing required. They can also be susceptible to mold infestation, which is associated with carcinogenic aflatoxins, and this can sometimes cause shortages on the global market.

Most of the world's pistachios are harvested in Iran, the United States (particularly California), and Turkey. European pistachios come predominantly from Greece, Spain, and Italy.

Unfortunately, our insatiable appetite for these nuts is threatening the survival of a plant that has been around for centuries. Due to overgrazing and excessive consumption, the International Union for Conservation of Nature has classified the pistachio as a near threatened species.

With this in mind, when buying pistachios, seek out high-quality, organically farmed produce, ideally from producers that are open about their cultivation and harvesting philosophy.

CULINARY USES

If you buy unshelled pistachios, you need to remember that you will lose roughly half the weight once they are shelled. Pistachios have a slightly sweet, aromatic, nutty flavor that works particularly well in mild dishes. Roasted chopped pistachios taste great sprinkled over fresh salads or creamy soups and add an exquisite touch to sweet dishes. They are also a popular snack and baking ingredient.

Main cultivation areas for pistachios

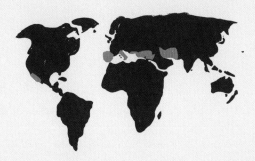

CAULIFLOWER STEAKS WITH PINEAPPLE RICE

VANILLA · CURRY POWDER · PUMPKIN SEED

Heat the coconut oil in a small saucepan until melted. Preheat the oven to 350°F (180°C) (convection setting). Line a baking sheet with parchment paper. Remove the pineapple from the soaking liquid, reserving the liquid. Purée with the coconut oil, turmeric, cardamom, vanilla powder, tamari, coconut sugar, chile flakes, and salt to create a spreadable paste — if it is too thick, add a bit of the reserved soaking liquid.

Remove the outer leaves and lower part of the stalk from the cauliflower then cut into roughly twelve pieces. Transfer to the lined baking sheet, brush liberally with the pineapple mixture, and bake for 20–30 minutes until crisp and brown.

Meanwhile, for the pineapple rice, wash the rice thoroughly in a bowl and drain in a sieve. Rinse the rice again then combine with the dried pineapple, curry powder, salt, and 1 ¼ cups (300 ml) of water in a medium saucepan and bring to a boil. Reduce the heat, cover the pan, and let the rice simmer gently for about 20 minutes until all the water has been absorbed.

Toast the pumpkin seeds in a small dry pan until they begin to pop.

Serve the pineapple rice with the baked cauliflower arranged on top. Drizzle with the pumpkin seed oil and sprinkle with the pumpkin seeds.

SERVES 4

Preparation time
45 minutes + 15 minutes soaking time + 20 minutes cooking time

Kitchen equipment
Freestanding or immersion blender

For the cauliflower steaks
· 4 tbsp coconut oil
· 2–3 ounces (60–90 g) dried pineapple, soaked in boiling water for 15 minutes
· ½ tsp each ground turmeric, ground cardamom, and bourbon vanilla powder
· 2 tbsp tamari soy sauce (strong, dark soy sauce)
· 2 tbsp coconut sugar
· 1 pinch chile flakes
· 1 pinch salt
· 1 large cauliflower

For the pineapple rice
· 1 cup (200 g) basmati rice
· 1 ¾ ounces (50 g) dried pineapple pieces or chunks
· 1 tsp curry powder
· ½ tsp salt

Also
· 4 tbsp pumpkin seeds
· 4 tbsp pumpkin seed oil

Tip:

If you prefer to serve slices of cauliflower steak, you can cut 2 thick slices from the center of each of two heads of cauliflower. The rest of the cauliflower can be used to make tabbouleh (recipe see p. 108/109) or soup (recipe see p. 157).

BAKED SQUASH ROUNDS WITH A GREEN SALSA

ARUGULA · MISO · HAZELNUT

SERVES 4

Preparation time
35 minutes

For the squash rounds
· 1 large butternut squash (with as long a "neck" as possible)
· olive oil
· 1 tsp chile flakes
· 1 tsp ground cinnamon
· salt
· freshly ground pepper

For the dressing
· ⅓ cup plus 2 tbsp (100 ml) hazelnut oil
· 5 tbsp mild apple cider vinegar (or wine vinegar)
· 2 tbsp light miso (shiro miso or lupine miso)
· 1–2 tbsp maple syrup
· 1 tsp mustard

For the salsa
· 1 bunch arugula leaves
· 1 bunch fresh parsley (or wild garlic or ramps, as soon as they are avaiable from March onwards)
· 1 lemon
· salt
· freshly ground pepper

Also
· 3 ½ ounces (100 g) roasted hazelnuts

Preheat the oven to 350°F (180°C) (convection setting). Grease a baking sheet. Cut the "neck" section of the butternut squash into four or eight thin round slices; use the rest of the squash for a different recipe (see tip). Transfer to the greased baking sheet, lightly brush with olive oil, and sprinkle with the chile flakes and cinnamon. Season with salt and pepper and bake for about 20 minutes until soft and beginning to brown.

Meanwhile, stir the hazelnut oil, apple cider vinegar, miso, maple syrup, and mustard together in a small bowl to make the dressing.

Finely chop the arugula leaves and parsley and transfer to a medium bowl. Zest and juice the lemon, add to the arugula and parsley, and toss to create a salsa. Season with salt and pepper.

Roughly chop the hazelnuts. Arrange the squash rounds on plates, drizzle with the dressing, scatter with the hazelnuts, and serve with the salsa.

Tastes great with:
Flat rice noodles or creamy polenta.

Tip:
The rest of the butternut squash can be used in the next few days to make soup (recipe see p. 205) or pumpkin spread with Brazil nuts (recipe see p. 154).

SAFFRON RISOTTO WITH PUNTARELLE

CASHEW & WHITE WINE CREAM · LEMON · MACADAMIA

SERVES 4

Preparation time
1 hour 15 minutes (+ about
30 minutes for the nut Parmesan)

Recipe photo see p. 220/221

Remove any blemished puntarelle leaves and cut off the lower part of the stalk. Separate the large leaves and set aside 6–8 of the best ones; use the remaining leaves for another recipe (see tip). Remove the core and break into separate pieces. Clean the 6–8 reserved leaves and cut diagonally into thin strips.

Zest and juice 1 of the lemons. Slice the other lemon as thinly as possible into rounds. In a medium bowl, toss the puntarelle leaves with the lemon juice, some salt, and 2 tablespoons of olive oil; set aside.

Peel and finely slice the garlic. Soak the saffron threads in 1 cup (240 ml) of warm water.

Heat 2 tablespoons of olive oil in a large saucepan and sauté the garlic and rice over moderate heat, stirring constantly, until the garlic starts to color and stick to the bottom of the pan. Deglaze the pan with the white wine, scraping any delicious bits from the bottom of the pan, and allow the liquid to be fully absorbed. Add the saffron and its soaking liquid (the threads will dissolve during cooking) and allow to be absorbed. Add about a third of the vegetable broth and bring to a boil. Reduce the heat to low, add the sliced lemon, and simmer gently, occasionally stirring and adding more vegetable broth as it's absorbed, until the rice is cooked.

Meanwhile, heat some olive oil in a small saucepan and sauté the pieces of the puntarelle core briskly over high heat. Add some water (or white wine), cover the pan, and steam over low heat for 3–5 minutes. Roughly chop the macadamia nuts.

Mix the cashew butter, white wine, salt, and ⅓ cup (80 ml) of hot water in a medium bowl to make the creamy cashew sauce. Stir this creamy sauce and the lemon zest into the risotto. Season with salt and pepper.

Divide the risotto between plates, arrange pieces of puntarelle in the center of each, and scatter the marinated puntarelle leaves on top. Sprinkle with the macadamias and nut Parmesan, if using, before serving.

Tip:

The rest of the puntarelle leaves will keep in the refrigerator for 2–3 days and can be added to salads or pan-fried in the same way as spinach or Swiss chard.

For the risotto

· 1 large head puntarelle (cicoria asparago)
· 2 lemons
· salt
· olive oil
· 1–2 garlic cloves
· a couple saffron threads
· 2 cups (400 g) Arborio rice
· ⅓ cup (80 ml) white wine, plus more if desired
· 2–2 ½ cups (480–600 ml) vegetable broth
· 3 ½ ounces (100 g) roasted macadamia nuts
· freshly ground pepper
· optional: nut Parmesan (basic recipe see p. 27), to taste

For the creamy cashew sauce

· ½ cup (100 g) cashew butter
· 2–3 tbsp white wine (or lemon juice)
· 1 tsp salt

NO CHEESE FONDUE

WHITE BEAN · CASHEW · MISO · PEPPER

Put the beans in a sieve and rinse with cold water. Blend the beans, cashew butter, yeast flakes, miso, mustard, salt, turmeric, and 2 cups (480 ml) of water into a smooth purée.

Peel and finely chop the garlic. In a small bowl, stir the tapioca flour with half of the white wine until smooth.

Heat some canola oil in a large saucepan and sauté the garlic over moderate heat until fragrant. Add the bean and cashew purée and bring to a boil, stirring constantly. Add the tapioca paste and simmer gently, stirring constantly, until the mixture is thick and leaves a ribbon trail when you lift out the spoon. Gradually stir in the rest of the white wine until you achieve the desired consistency. Season with pepper and possibly more white wine and transfer to a fondue dish.

Dip the cubes of baguette or small potatoes using fondue forks and enjoy. Stir the creamy mix every so often, so it doesn't stick to the bottom.

Tastes great with:
A winter side salad and a glass of white wine.

SERVES 4 TO 8

Preparation time
45 minutes

Kitchen equipment
Freestanding or immersion blender

Ingredients
· 5 ¼ ounces (150 g) canned or jarred white beans (drained weight)
· ½ cup (100 g) cashew butter
· ⅓ cup (20 g) nutritional yeast flakes
· 1 heaping tbsp rice miso (or lupin miso)
· 1 tsp spicy mustard
· 1 tsp salt
· 1 pinch ground turmeric
· 1 garlic clove
· 3 tbsp tapioca flour (or cornstarch)
· about ¾ cup (180 ml) dry white wine
· canola oil
· freshly ground white pepper
· cubes of baguette or small potatoes

WINTER NUT ROAST WITH CHESTNUTS

MUSHROOM · CELERY · CASHEW · THYME

SERVES 6 TO 8

Preparation time
1 hour 20 minutes
+ 35 minutes baking time
+ 15 minutes resting time

Kitchen equipment
Freestanding blender, hand mixer
or stand mixer, approx. 12 × 4-inch
(30 × 10 cm) loaf pan

Recipe photo see p. 226/227

In a small bowl, stir the psyllium husks into ¾ cup (180 ml) of water and leave to swell until ready to use. Clean and chop the button mushrooms. Finely slice the celery. Peel the celeriac then finely grate or dice. Heat some olive oil in a large pan. Add the mushrooms and sauté briskly over high heat, then add the celery and celeriac and continue cooking for a few minutes until the vegetables start to brown. Deglaze the pan with 4 tablespoons of the tamari, scraping any delicious bits from the bottom of the pan, then stir in the tomato paste. Remove from the heat, cover the pan, and keep warm until ready to use.

Grind the dried mushrooms to make mushroom powder. Add the cashews and chop roughly. Transfer to a large bowl. Peel and finely chop the garlic. Add to the dried mushroom and cashew mixture, along with the buckwheat flakes, chestnuts, yeast flakes, thyme, ½ teaspoon of salt, and the prunes, if using. Stir well to combine. Add the red wine, the remaining 2 tablespoons of tamari, and the mushroom and vegetable mixture from the pan and mix well. Work in the soaked psyllium husks by hand, making sure everything is well combined, or use the dough hook attachment on a hand mixer or stand mixer until you have a mixture that will keep its shape. Work in the lupin flour, if using, to help the mixture bind together. Season with salt.

Preheat the oven to 350°F (180°C) (convection setting). Line the loaf pan with parchment paper, leaving a 1-inch (2.5 cm) overhang on the long sides. To make the glaze, stir together the olive oil, tamari, maple syrup, salt, and paprika in a small bowl. Transfer the nut roast mixture to the loaf pan, press it down with the back of a spoon, and brush with half of the glaze. Bake, occasionally brushing the top with more glaze, for 35–40 minutes until the surface has browned slightly. Turn the oven off but let the nut roast rest inside for 15 minutes. Carefully lift the nut roast out of the pan using the parchment paper and slice with a sharp knife for serving.

Tastes great with:

Mashed potatoes, a gratin, or sliced and served cold on bread the next day.

For the nut roast

- ⅔ cup (50 g) ground psyllium husks
- 7 ounces (200 g) button mushrooms (or oyster mushrooms)
- 3 ½ ounces (100 g) celery
- 3 ½ ounces (100 g) celeriac (or parsley root)
- olive oil
- 6 tbsp tamari soy sauce (strong, dark soy sauce)
- 2 tbsp tomato paste
- ¾ ounce (20 g) dried mushrooms
- 7 ounces (200 g) cashew pieces (or mixed nuts)
- 2 garlic cloves
- 3 ½ ounces (100 g) buckwheat flakes (milled buckwheat groats)
- 3 ½ ounces (100 g) cooked chestnuts
- ⅔ cup (40 g) nutritional yeast flakes
- 1 tbsp dried thyme
- salt
- optional: 1 ¾ ounces (50 g) prunes
- 4 tbsp red wine (or tomato passata)
- optional: ½ cup (60 g) lupin flour (or soy flour)

For the glaze

- ⅓ cup (80 ml) olive oil
- ⅓ cup (80 ml) tamari soy sauce (strong, dark soy sauce)
- 4 tbsp maple syrup
- ½ tsp salt
- 1 pinch smoked paprika (such as Pimentón de la Vera)

THE CHESTNUT

From a botanical perspective, chestnuts, also known as sweet chestnuts, are a type of nut. However, they differ from other kinds of nuts and not just in appearance.

The **sweet chestnut tree** belongs to the Fagaceae or beech family and is a deciduous tree that grows to a height of 115 feet (35 meters). It loves warmth and grows mainly on mountainous terrain in temperate Mediterranean areas. It does not like conditions to be too wet or too dry. Chestnuts were being cultivated as a source of wood and food in the mountain regions of southern Europe as far back as medieval times. The edible fruit was a staple food for rural populations up to the late 19th century.

Chestnut trees do not blossom until the relatively mature age of 20 to 25 years (cultivars blossom slightly earlier) and only then do they produce their starchy nuts. Edible chestnuts are subdivided into three types — chestnuts, sweet chestnuts (also called **marroni**), and late-harvested chestnuts — which each differ slightly in appearance and taste. Sweet chestnuts have the best flavor and are usually the most widely available.

Each **chestnut** grows in a prickly, green husk. As the chestnuts ripen, the prickles dry out and turn brown then the husk splits open and the nut is released. In wild varieties, the husk is generally small and contains just a single chestnut, while in cultivated varieties, it is larger and contains up to three nuts. These edible seeds are enclosed in a thin skin and a leathery brown shell that is not completely hard. This shell cannot be cracked but must be slit open to access the nut inside.

Untreated chestnuts do not keep long, because their high starch content causes them to rot quickly. This is why the nuts are fermented, dried, frozen, smoked, or treated with gas to make them more durable.

HEALTH BENEFITS

Chestnuts have an interesting nutrient profile. Unlike other nuts, they contain hardly any fat (only about 2 percent), roughly 3 percent protein, and lots of complex carbohydrates (about 40 percent). The protein is free from prolamins and glutenins, which is why chestnuts and chestnut flour are ideal for a gluten-free diet.

These nuts also contain impressive quantities of essential amino acids. With an Omega-6 to Omega-3 fatty acid ratio of 7:1, chestnuts have one of the best scores of any nut, alongside walnuts, which have a ratio of 6:1 — the ideal fatty acid ratio is 5:1. This is another characteristic that has always made chestnuts such a valuable ingredient. They also supply lots of potassium, vitamins C and E, and all the B vitamins. Chestnuts thus make an excellent addition to the menu for anyone following a plant-based diet.

ECONOMIC CHALLENGES

Sweet chestnuts are grown in many regions of the world, but they are particularly common and produce a large crop in warmer parts of southern and western Europe. China is the largest producer, followed by Spain, Bolivia, Turkey, South Korea, Italy, and Portugal. Switzerland and South Africa also have lots of small local chestnut businesses that sell their product exclusively at a regional level.

The chestnut tree population is under threat particularly from chestnut blight and ink disease, which causes root rot due to infestation by the Phytophthora fungus.

CULINARY USES

Chestnuts should not be consumed raw and only acquire their delicately sweet, nutty flavor after cooking or roasting. Their distinctive taste and slightly floury consistency go beautifully with mushrooms in a creamy almond sauce, in nut roasts, or as a garnish for braised cabbage. Roasted chestnuts are a hugely popular snack during the winter months.

Chestnut flour is a highly versatile baking ingredient — both for savory breads and sweet items. Healthy sweet treats can be rustled up by using chestnut purée.

Main cultivation areas for chestnuts

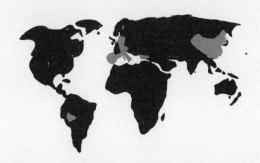

CHRISTMAS FLAN WITH PLUMS IN PORT

CHESTNUT · DATE · PUMPKIN SPICE · ALMOND

SERVES 8

Preparation time

50 minutes + overnight soaking
+ 8 hours cooling time

Kitchen equipment

Freestanding or immersion
blender, 8 small ramekins

For the flan

· 7 ounces (200 g) cooked chestnuts
· 3 ½ ounces (100 g) dates, pitted
  and soaked in water overnight
· 2 cups (480 ml) vanilla soy milk
· 1 pinch salt
· 1 pinch pumpkin spice or
  speculoos spice
· optional: maple syrup
· 2 ½ tbsp cornstarch
· 1 tsp agar-agar

For the plums in port

· 14 ounces (400 g) canned plums
· 4 tbsp port
· 1 cinnamon stick (or some ground
  cinnamon)

Also

· 1 ¾ ounces (50 g) almonds

Roughly chop the chestnuts. Remove the dates from their soaking liquid and blend with half the soy milk, the chestnuts, salt, and a pinch of pumpkin spice until very smooth. Add more spice, if desired, and maple syrup, if using — the mixture should have an intense Christmas spice flavor and taste sweet but not excessively so. Stir in the cornstarch and agar-agar.

Heat the rest of the soy milk in a large saucepan. As soon as the liquid simmers, stir in the prepared mixture with a balloon whisk. Simmer over moderate heat, stirring constantly to prevent sticking, for 1–2 minutes until thick. Transfer the hot flan mixture to the ramekins and let cool slightly. Refrigerate for at least 8 hours to set.

Drain the plums in a sieve, reserving the liquid. In a medium saucepan, simmer the plums with the port and cinnamon stick, occasionally adding some of the reserved liquid to prevent burning, for 25–30 minutes until almost falling apart.

Meanwhile, toast the almonds in a small dry pan over moderate heat then chop roughly.

Slip a thin knife around the edge of each flan to loosen it, then turn out onto a dessert plate. Top with the warm poached plums, sprinkle with the almonds, and serve.

Tastes great with:

*A dollop of the date and almond cream
(recipe see p. 237).*

MARZIPAN COOKIES WITH DATE AND ALMOND CREAM

ORANGE · SILKEN TOFU · CINNAMON

Preheat the oven to 350°F (180°C) (convection setting). Line two baking sheets with parchment paper. Finely grate the marzipan for the cookies. Beat the raw cane sugar and margarine in a large bowl until light and fluffy. Stir in the marzipan, almond butter, and salt, then add the flour and stir just enough to create a fine crumbly texture. Remove 8–10 tablespoons of this mixture and set aside. Add the oat milk and orange zest to the remaining crumble mixture and stir for about 1 minute to create a creamy but stiff dough.

Using two damp teaspoons, scoop round ping pong ball–sized portions of the dough and transfer to the lined baking sheets, making sure the cookies are slightly spread out. Make an indentation in the center of each cookie and sprinkle in some of the reserved crumbs. Bake for about 15 minutes until golden, then let cool slightly on the baking sheets.

Purée the dates with their soaking liquid. Add the tofu, almond butter, cinnamon, and salt and continue processing until smooth and creamy.

Serve the marzipan cookies with the almond and date cream.

MAKES ABOUT 16 COOKIES

Preparation time
1 hour + overnight soaking

Kitchen equipment
Hand mixer or stand mixer, freestanding or immersion blender

For the cookies
· 3 ½ ounces (100 g) marzipan
· ⅓ cup (65 g) raw cane sugar
· ⅓ cup (80 g) vegan margarine (at room temperature)
· 4 ¼ ounces (120 g) almond butter
· 1 pinch salt
· 2 ¾ cups to 3 1/3 cups (250–300 g) (gluten-free) oat flour (or white spelt flour)
· ½ cup (120 ml) oat milk
· 2 tbsp orange zest

For the date and almond cream
· 3 ½ ounces (100 g) dates, pitted and soaked in a small amount of water overnight
· 7 ounces (200 g) silken tofu (or soy yogurt)
· ½ cup (100 g) almond butter
· 1 pinch ground cinnamon
· 1 pinch salt

Tip:
The almond and date cream also tastes fantastic as a substitute for whipped cream served with apple pie, pancakes, fruit salad, or flan (recipe see p. 234).

PEANUT AND PINEAPPLE LEBKUCHEN

DATE · COCOA BUTTER

MAKES ABOUT 12 LEBKUCHEN

Preparation time
1 hour 15 minutes

Kitchen equipment
Hand mixer or stand mixer

For the lebkuchen
- 4 ¾ ounces (130 g) peanuts
- 3 ½ ounces (100 g) dates, pitted
- 1 ¼ ounces (40 g) dried pineapple
- 2 tsp lebkuchen spice mix (or gingerbread spice mix)
- 1 pinch salt
- optional: lemon zest (or orange zest)
- 1 ounce (30 g) cocoa butter (or coconut oil)
- 2 ¾ ounces (80 g) peanut butter
- 3–4 tbsp lupin flour (or soy flour)
- round german baking wafers (oblaten), 2–3 inches (5–8 cm) in diameter (or rice paper, cut to size)

For the glaze
- 1 ¾ ounces (50 g) peanuts
- 1 ounce (30 g) cocoa butter (or coconut oil)
- 1 ¾ ounces (50 g) peanut butter
- 2 tbsp maple syrup (or coconut sugar)
- 2 tbsp good quality cocoa powder

Finely chop the peanuts for the lebkuchen mix. Chop the dates into small pieces and finely shred the dried pineapple. Combine the peanuts, dates, and pineapple with the lebkuchen spice mix and salt in a large bowl. Add the lemon zest, if using.

Melt the cocoa butter in a bowl suspended over a pan of simmering water. Add to the dry ingredients, along with the peanut butter, and use the dough hook attachment to combine. Gradually work in the lupin flour until the dough comes together and holds its shape. Knead once again by hand until smooth and elastic. Use a teaspoon to spread the mix evenly over the baking wafers.

Roughly chop the peanuts for the glaze. Once again, melt the cocoa butter in a bowl suspended over a pan of simmering water. Combine with the peanut butter and maple syrup in a medium bowl and stir until smooth. Add the cocoa powder and beat until creamy. Spread this over the lebkuchen, scatter with the peanuts, and refrigerate to set the glaze.

Tip:
Store the lebkuchen in an airtight container in a cool, dry location and they will keep for at least 3–4 weeks.

Quick and easy:
Lebkuchen spice mix

Lebkuchen spice mix is similar to gingerbread spice mix and can easily be made at home. Combine 2 ½ tbsp ground cinnamon, 2 tsp ground cloves, and ½ tsp each of ground allspice, ground coriander, ground green cardamom, ground ginger, ground star anise, ground mace, and ground nutmeg. Store in an airtight container for all your holiday baking needs.

SEEDS

Crunchy seeds are popular all over the world and have always been an important part of our diet.

SUNFLOWER SEEDS

Sunflowers originally come from northern and central America and were brought to Europe by Spanish sailors in the mid-sixteenth century. From the 17th century onwards, the flat, slightly tapered seeds were used for baking or as a substitute for coffee or drinking chocolate. In modern cooking, they are mainly used to make sunflower oil.

As much as **sunflower seeds** themselves are healthy — they are an excellent source of folic acid and magnesium — the oil extracted from them is less good for us. Both the seeds and the oil contain almost exclusively unsaturated fats, and certainly far too much linoleic acid, which means they have a poor ratio of Omega-6 to Omega-3 fatty acids. You won't exceed the critical quantity by eating the whole seeds because it would be unusual to consume more than ¾ to 1 ½ ounces (20 to 45 grams) in one go. On the other hand, if you use sunflower oil for salad dressings or marinades, for roasting or frying, to emulsify mayonnaise or spreads, and so on, you can easily use considerable quantities, which can then completely imbalance the body's Omega-6 and Omega-3 levels. Consequently, whole sunflower seeds get a thumbs up, but it is best to use canola or olive oil instead of sunflower oil.

The sunflower seeds available in shops come mainly from Russia, Ukraine, Argentina, Romania, and China. When shopping, try to source seeds from your local area.

In cooking, sunflower seeds add a crunchy texture to savory dishes and have a delicately nutty, slightly bitter taste. You can roast them to enhance any salad or use ground seeds to make the pastry for a quiche more interesting.

PUMPKIN SEEDS

You can eat the seeds from all edible **pumpkins**. Particularly delicious seeds can be found in the Cucurbita pepo varieties (field pumpkins) and the Lady Godiva pumpkin (also known as oil squash). These have less flesh and contain soft seeds, which have not developed a hard exterior and thus can be used without first being hulled.

Pumpkins originate from central and south America, but nowadays are grown around the world. Most of the pumpkin seeds sold come from China, Ukraine, Russia, Spain, Mexico, and the United States. To promote regional trade and reduce transportation, it is important for all consumers to look for local produce when shopping.

Pumpkin seeds have a protein content of about 25 percent, which makes these flat, dark green seeds a particularly welcome source of protein for those following a plant-based diet. In addition, they are rich in magnesium and iron and contain lots of B vitamins and vitamin E.

In cooking, roasted pumpkin seeds are the ideal crunchy addition to salads and vegetable dishes, or they can be caramelized slightly for use in desserts. Pumpkin seed oil makes salad dressings and marinades turn dark green in color and introduces a mild but unique flavor. It is particularly popular combined with vanilla ice cream — it might sound strange, but it tastes fantastic!

243

SESAME SEEDS

The seeds from the **sesame plant** are one of the oilseeds that have been cultivated for the longest time. The plants originate from southern Asia but have spread rapidly through tropical and sub-tropical regions and are now widely used, particularly in Asian, Indian, and Middle Eastern cuisine. The largest sesame seed producers include Sudan, Myanmar, India, and Tanzania.

Sesame seeds are pale beige, light brown, or black, although the black variety are often harder to find in shops. They are a good plant-based source of protein, with a protein content of about 17 percent; are rich in calcium, magnesium, potassium, and iron; and contain some B vitamins plus vitamin E. The fat in these little seeds consists mostly of monounsaturated and polyunsaturated fatty acids.

In Japan, these tart and slightly bitter seeds are used to make a popular aromatic spice mix (gomashio). Sesame seeds are also used to enhance savory baked goods and are great for making a delicious coating (nut rissoles, recipe see p. 210). Tahini, which is a sesame seed paste, is an ingredient used in lots of sauces and dips, including hummus. In Middle Eastern desserts and other sweet treats, sesame seeds are often combined with vanilla, cinnamon, and cardamom.

FLAXSEED

The **flax plant** belongs to the Linaceae family and is cultivated to produce oil. The seeds it produces are popular all over the world. The main cultivation areas for this plant (also known as **linseed**) are North America, especially Canada, along with Russia, Kazakhstan, China, India, and Ethiopia. The largest European producers include Great Britain and France.

Flat, brown **flaxseeds** contain roughly 37 percent fat and have a very high proportion of linolenic acid (Omega-3 fatty acid), an essential unsaturated fatty acid often lacking in our diets. Flaxseeds also contain exceptionally high levels of micronutrients and plenty of fiber. The mucilage in the seeds stimulates peristalsis and thus improves digestion. That is why I thoroughly recommend including 1–2 tbsp of flaxseed meal in your daily diet.

Flaxseeds have a nutty, aromatic flavor, and an absorbent nature that makes them an ideal ingredient for overnight oats, as well as sweet and savory loaves. They can also be used as a substitute for eggs in baking — use 3 tbsp of flaxseed meal soaked in ¼ cup (60 ml) of water for each egg in cake mix, pancake batter, or other recipes as a binding agent and to improve the overall nutritional balance.

HEMP SEEDS

The brown or greenish grey seeds from the **hemp plant** are a real miracle of nature. Hemp originates from Asia and, along with flax and sesame, is one of the oldest cultivated plants. The seeds are a rich source of nutrients and have all sorts of culinary uses, but components from the plants are also used for house building and to make fabric. In China, hemp seeds continue to be one of the most important staple foods today. The main cultivation areas are China, Russia, Canada, and France, but commercial hemp production has also been found in other regions for many decades. When you are shopping, it is important to check the product's country of origin and try to buy from local producers.

Hemp seeds provide lots of magnesium, calcium, potassium, iron, zinc, manganese, some sulfur, and vitamin E, plus a large variety of B vitamins. Like flaxseeds and walnuts, they are an excellent source of Omega-3 fatty acids.

Milled whole hemp seeds are a fabulously aromatic baking ingredient to add to loaves and bread rolls. Hulled hemp seeds have an intense, nutty flavor that works well in either sweet or savory dishes and adds a certain something to salads, vegetable dishes, and other recipes, as well as incorporating lots of valuable nutrients.

MY PANTRY ESSENTIALS AND EQUIPMENT FOR EVERYDAY COOKING

To make sure we are talking the same culinary language, I'm going to let you peek inside my pantry to see what foods I always have in stock in addition to fresh fruit, vegetables, and herbs. I will also reveal which practical kitchen items I use for my everyday cooking.

MY PANTRY ESSENTIALS

Let's start with the lead characters in this book: **nuts**, **nut butters**, and **seeds**. In addition to a supply of **pumpkin seeds, sunflower seeds,** and **flaxseeds**, which I have ready to roast for soups or salads or for baking, I always have some unsalted, unroasted nuts in stock — preferably **Brazil nuts** (for my daily selenium intake) and **almonds** (just because they are a delicious snack). For salad dressings and to round off various other dishes, the ingredients I most often turn to are **tahini**, **blended nut butters**, and **peanut butter**. Nuts and nut butters never last more than four weeks with me, which is why I always have such a good supply.

I love sauces with lots of flavor and hearty dishes with plenty of umami. For **salad dressings** and **marinades**, I always have a bottle of mild **apple cider vinegar** and a more rounded **white balsamic vinegar**. In summer, I add a high-quality, mature **balsamic vinegar**, which I love to drizzle over colorful tomatoes. Occasionally I treat myself to a delicious **raspberry vinegar**.

There is always some **extra-virgin olive oil** in my kitchen and a bottle of **flaxseed oil** in my fridge. For brisk sautéing, I also like to use **coconut oil**. I only buy **pumpkin seed oil**, **walnut oil**, and **hazelnut oil** when I really need them or want to try something new, because they go rancid very quickly. For a rounded walnut or hazelnut flavor, I prefer to use the whole nuts or some nut butter.

Soy sauce (in my case, gluten-free **tamari**), sweet **rice wine (mirin)**, and a mild **rice vinegar (genmai su)** add an Asian touch to my array of condiments. I also love to use **ume su**, which is a slightly tart and salty seasoning sauce made from umeboshi, which are pickled apricots.

Spices have an even greater significance for me because they do more than just contribute flavor. I know a bit about the medicinal power attributed to spices in Ayurvedic and traditional Chinese medicine, and even by Hildegard von Bingen. That is why I think it is so important to focus on high-quality spices and use them with love, mindfulness, and appreciation. I put all my spices in small, airtight jars and make sure I use them promptly, as spices do not keep indefinitely. They lose their flavor and color, and no doubt also their health-giving properties.

My basic kit includes **salt** (especially **sea salt** and **rock salt**) and **pepper** (**black**, **white**, and **Kampot**) but also **turmeric**, **sweet paprika**, **cayenne pepper**, ground and whole **cumin**, mild **curry powder**, **aniseeds**, **fennel** and **coriander seeds**, **yellow** and **black mustard seeds**, plus **asafetida** (as used in Indian cuisine). I like to use Himalayan **black salt (kala namak)**, and sometimes **smoked salt** and **smoked paprika** to add a slight "eggy" flavor or a hint of smoke to a dip.

I always have miso paste for seasoning in my refrigerator. The most versatile product is a pale **shiro miso** made from rice and soybeans. I also love lupin miso and the more powerful, dark **hatcho miso**.

To add a bit more depth to certain dishes, I like using **mustard (whole-grain, medium-hot, and spicy)** and **nutritional yeast flakes**. Yeast flakes are rich in vitamin B, so they are an excellent nutritional supplement, but they also taste fantastic.

Grains such as **millet**, **Arborio rice**, and **buckwheat** are essential pantry items. I only buy other types of grain if I am planning to use them imminently. For spontaneous baking, I also like to have **oats**, **buckwheat flour**, and **rice flour**. **Chestnut flour** and a **gluten-free flour** round out my **flour supplies**.

There is usually some **pasta** made from grains or pulses in my cupboard — I just keep a small quantity on hand, only buying more once I have used it all up.

In terms of dried **pulses**, I always have **yel-low** and **red lentils**, plus some **Beluga lentils** in my kitchen — they cook quickly and are ideal for thickening soups. **White beans** are another vital item (these are my favorite).

As a **last-minute** option, I always recommend having a high-quality **pesto** in your pantry, which you can use to rustle up an easy pasta dish or to add flavor to stir-fried vegetables. You should also have a jar or can of **sweet corn**, plus several jars or cans of **cooked pulses** and **white beans** for a quick hummus or other dip. It's also useful to have a couple jars of vegan vegetable **spreads** and **pastes**, which you will find in health food stores. These ingredients make it easy to be cre-ative with your leftovers, transforming yester-day's rice, potatoes, or cooked vegetables into a delicious bowl of food.

MY EQUIPMENT ESSENTIALS

I generally only use two **knives**: one large **chef's knife** and a small **paring knife**, perhaps to remove a stalk or any woody sections. Make sure both knives are sharp, as well as comfort-able to hold and easy to guide as you cut.

I like to chop things on a large **wood-en board**. I am not personally a fan of plastic chopping surfaces. There are hygienic reasons for favoring wood because it doesn't produce any harmful microparticles, and certain kinds of wood even have antibacterial properties.

For grating and slicing fruit and vegetables, I own a **grater** and a **mandoline**. My utensils drawer also has a **vegetable peeler**, **balloon whisk**, various **wooden spoons**, and a **can opener**.

I like to cook using **large saucepans** and **skillets** to make sure there is plenty of room to toss whatever I am cooking or frying. Two saucepans and a skillet are all you need for everyday use. Of course, you will need more pans if you regularly cook for friends and family and want to offer your guests several courses.

The most important pieces of **electri-cal kitchen equipment** for everyday use are probably my **powerful food processor** and my **freestanding blender**. It chops nuts and seeds, makes incredibly creamy soups, and smoothly combines all sorts of ingredients. I occasionally use an **immersion blender** to froth up some nut butter and warm water to make a quick almond milk for my coffee or to blend a salad dressing or pesto sauce. In other words, I use it when I'm working with quantities that are too small for my food processor to handle.

In general, the only baking I do at home is my spiced oat and hemp seed bread (recipe see p. 152) and the occasional cake or banana bread. I use a wooden spoon or **hand mixer** to combine the ingredients. I don't often knead yeasted doughs, which means my **stand mixer** doesn't get used that regularly and is not one of my essential kitchen gadgets. But, if you bake bread or cakes on a weekly basis, you will definitely benefit from having this kind of mixer for kneading and whisking.

My **baking equipment** also includes a **springform pan**, a **muffin pan** and **a loaf pan** — as you'll see in the recipes, I favor a longer loaf pan that measures 12 × 4-inch (30 × 10 cm).

For **storing** leftover food or ingredients from the zero-waste store, I use large **storage jars** and **food storage boxes**. I don't have any aluminum foil, plastic wrap, or an equivalent in my kitchen — if I need to cover something I just use plates or some **vegan wax wraps**. Even **parchment paper** is something I use sparingly because its nonstick coating means it cannot be recycled.

INDEX

THE MOST IMPORTANT NUTS AND SEEDS

THE MOST IMPORTANT FRESH INGREDIENTS

Lena Kaltenbach (digital operator), Vera Guala (stylist), Estella Schweizer (author), Winfried Heinze (photographer)

ACKNOWLEDGMENTS

Cooking and baking with nuts has been a key part of my daily routine for years — it's been a lifelong passion that began with almond butter on my morning toast. And from an early age, I unknowingly benefitted from the culinary value and special nutritional properties of nuts and seeds.

Ever since I started working at fairfood Freiburg — a German company that sells fair trade and organic nuts and nut products, as well as advocates for sustainable production — and learned more about the complex trading relationships around nuts, I knew I wanted to write a cookbook that puts those nutritional superstars center stage — a book that would be enlightening, informative, inspirational, and enjoyable.

I specifically want to dedicate this book to all the producers around the world that cultivate or market organically certified, fair trade nuts — they are doing fantastic work and making a valuable contribution towards keeping nuts on the menu.

I also want to dedicate this book to companies like fairfood Freiburg, which promote fair trade markets in the Global North, in order to offer guaranteed sales for producers in the Global South, and thus support their livelihoods.

I want to thank all the consumers, employers, producers, and restaurant owners who shop for organic, fair trade produce, who check the country of origin, and who appreciate that it is worth paying a bit extra for environmentally friendly, sustainable, and profitable goods.

Thank you to Vera Guala for the unique and incredibly beautiful props, not to mention the expert and creative food styling. Thank you to Winfried Heinze, Lena Kaltenbach, and the whole team at b.lateral for their photography and design expertise. Thank you to Vera and Winfried for recognizing the potential of my nut book concept right from the start, and for sharing this journey together.

Thank you to Julie Kiefer for the knowledge and passion she has brought to coordinating the development of this book, and for always being so receptive to our various layout and design requests.

Thank you to Sabrina Kiefer for her fantastic editorial work and project management, and for understanding the kinds of recipes I wanted to create and share.

Thank you to Alison Tunley for the English translation, and to Lauren Salkeld for editing the English edition.

Let's go nuts about nuts!

ESTELLA SCHWEIZER is an expert vegan nutritionist, a certified plant-based chef, and one of Germany's top vegan cooks. Having run a vegan café in Regensburg, she now works as a recipe and product developer for fairfood Freiburg and other sustainable food start-ups. She helps restaurants and hotels develop climate-friendly recipe concepts and is part of the Good Food Collective. She also campaigns for sustainable nut production and trade.

WINFRIED HEINZE is a food photographer and co-director of b.lateral, a creative agency. He lives on Lake Constance in Germany, as well as London and Zurich, and works all around the world. His photos frequently appear in magazines, books, and other publications.

VERA GUALA, a prop and food stylist, was previously involved in screen printing in Bern, then trend analysis in Paris, before studying fashion in Zurich. Color and aesthetics have always played a key part in her working life, but she now focuses her skills primarily on the culinary and lifestyle domains.

B.TEAM are members of the b.lateral creative agency, and contributed with incredible love and skill, from the initial concept of the book to the final artwork. Hannes Knab, Rebecca Wiebel, and David Capó Valbona were responsible for the cover design, illustrations, typography, and layout, while Lena Kaltenbach used her expertise to perfect the photographic images in her role as digital operator. They all live on Lake Constance.

© Prestel Verlag,
Munich · London · New York, 2022
A member of Penguin Random House
Verlagsgruppe GmbH
Neumarkter Strasse 28 · 81673 Munich

Library of Congress Control Number is available; a CIP catalogue record for this book is available from the British Library.

Editorial direction: Julie Kiefer
Project management: Sabrina Kiefer
Translation from German: Alison Tunley
Copyediting: Lauren Salkeld
Design and layout: b.lateral creative agency
Production management: Corinna Pickart
Separations: Schnieber Graphik GmbH, Munich
Printing and binding: DZS GRAFIK, d.o.o.
Paper: Magno Natural

MIX
Paper from responsible sources
FSC® C106600

Penguin Random House Verlagsgruppe
FSC® N001967

Climate neutral
Print product
ClimatePartner.com/14044-1912-1001

Printed in Slovenia
ISBN 978-3-7913-8837-3
www.prestel.com

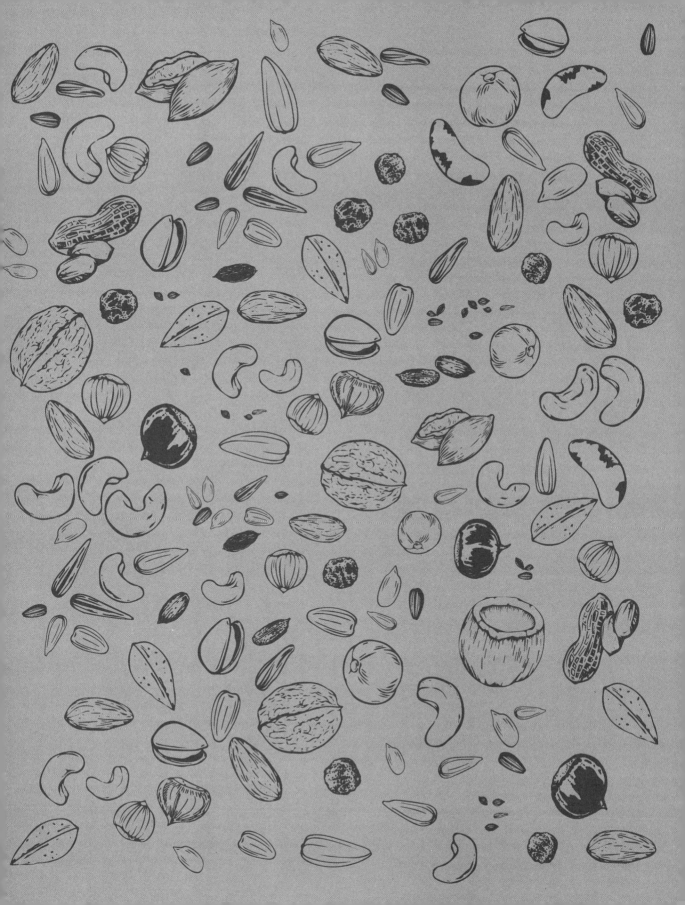

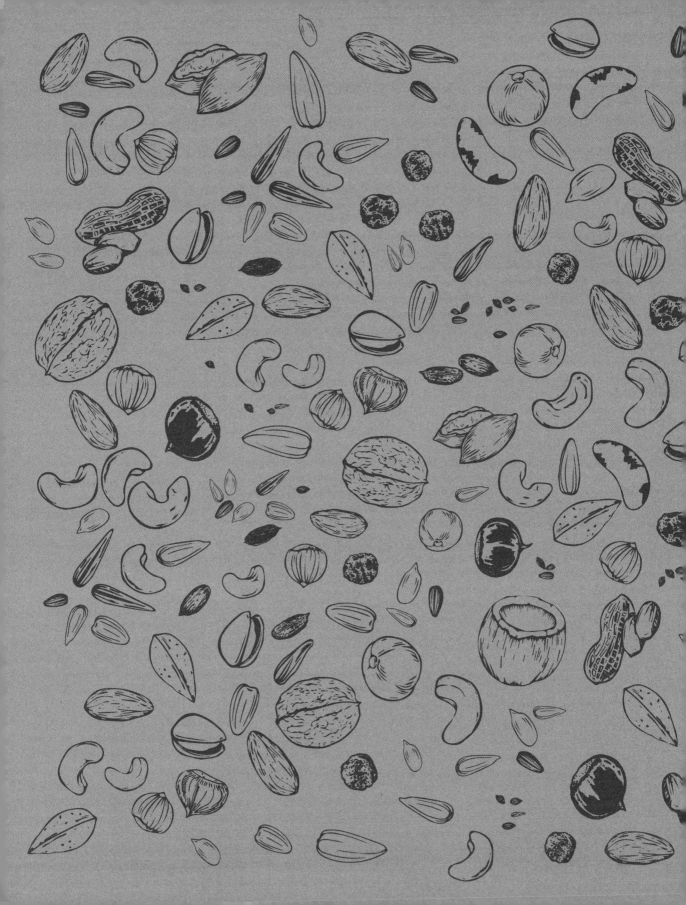